(19)

START
AT THE
END

START
AT THE
END

How Reverse-Engingeering
Can Lead to Success

DAN BIGHAM

WELBECK

Published by Welbeck
An imprint of Welbeck Non-Fiction Limited,
part of Welbeck Publishing Group.
Based in London and Sydney

First published by Welbeck in 2021

A CIP catalogue record for this book is available from the British Library

ISBN
Paperback – 9781802790733
eBook - 9781787396098

Typeset by seagulls.net
Printed and bound in the UK

10 9 8 7 6 5 4 3 2 1

www.welbeckpublishing.com

To all those who face an insurmountable challenge.

Contents

Introduction
The end

I settled myself on my bike. Took a few deep breaths whilst staring at the wooden track in front of me. The crowd were just a murmur in the background; so too the arena announcer reading out the names of my three team-mates lined up beside me. In front of us a digital clock counted down the seconds. I knew we were ready for this. All the months of training and planning, of sacrifice and stress, it was all going to come down to the next four minutes. In the unlikely setting of an arena on the outskirts of Minsk, Belarus, we were going to achieve our ambition.

This is the story of a track racing team – that intense indoor racing that can make you dizzy when you watch it on television. It is a high-speed, slightly bonkers sport with multiple disciplines, some simple, but some so baffling that even the referees (known as commissaires) get confused. And it is a sport that Britain has excelled at, from sprinter Reg Harris in the fifties, to Chris Boardman in the nineties and the bucketloads of Olympic gold medals won since Beijing 2008.

We were a bit different though. We are British but we were not with the Great Britain Cycling Team. We did it our own way, outside the system. We beat teams with far bigger budgets and resources, the national teams who have traditionally dominated the sport.

To get my team to this level I took a new approach to the sport. Shook things up a bit. Now I am working with some of the top professional and national teams. They want me to help them go faster. They want to know how we did it. And I think, finally, that everyone should know.

* * *

If you have an ambition, how do you become successful? The orthodoxy is that you must follow the system, work hard and persevere. In every part of our lives, whether in sport, business or education, there is a highly evolved system for filtering and developing talented individuals. Often the selection process begins when we are children. We are forced to assimilate into these systems, to work to their rules, to share their goals. We are told it always pays to follow the system.

But what if you find your passion late in life? What if, for whatever reason, you never even get into the system? Or you are kicked out of the system because you don't fit in? Should you just give up?

No, and here is why.

Scratch the surface and you will find that these highly evolved systems are not quite as evolved as they appear. They have been built over time, and it pays not to confuse time with intellectual rigour. Every hierarchical system based on performance contains some element of complacency, of lazy thinking and of vested interest. And that means that these systems can be beaten.

There is another way to success. And I'm going to share it with you. On my team's journey I have learnt a lot about why knowledge is more important than talent, about disruption and commitment and teamwork. I have applied these ideas to pedalling a bicycle but they can be applied to other parts of life too. Wherever you need to use your brain and your relationships to achieve something, at work or study, or even at home with your family, these ideas can help. My team-mates and I were not robotic elite athletes. I have learnt that being yourself is central to success. For example, at medal presentations, usually a pretty formal and dull affair, we wore cowboy hats. It was daft, it was different – it was me.

In this book we are going to examine each step of my journey towards success, show you how I plotted the road to success, and draw out the ideas that will help you achieve your own ambitions. This is not a shortcut, nor is it a hack (though it is used by computer hackers). It is a new way of thinking about how to become successful. It is called reverse engineering, and it changed our lives.

Part 1
Set your goal

1

Four minutes from history

Early evening, 6 May 1954. At the Iffley Road running track in the centre of Oxford, six young men line up for the blue riband event of distance running, the Mile. After a worryingly rainy and windy afternoon, the conditions have calmed and 3,000 people line the stands. Anticipation is high. The crowd already know who will win the race. What they're interested in is the winning time. The favourite is a 25-year-old medical student who ran his first mile race on this very track, seven years earlier, as a student at Exeter College. Today he knows history is within his grasp. He has prepared meticulously. Before travelling up from London by train, he rubbed graphite on his running spikes to prevent them picking up too much cinder ash.

I often used to think about Roger Bannister's world record when I was studying, and running, in Oxford. If you are a track runner in Oxford it is hard to dodge its shadow, especially if you frequently cycle past the Iffley Road track, as I did. Breaking four minutes for the mile became such an iconic symbol for sporting excellence, for the ability of man to train his body for a specific feat.

Bannister started running at 17, and though he showed talent he was initially lackadaisical about training. As he began to take his sport more seriously his times fell, results accumulated and the Olympics came into sight. Working with legendary Austrian coach Franz Stampfl, Bannister adopted what were regarded as ultra-modern 'scientific' training methods. Intervals – repeated high-intensity bursts with periods of recovery between – were central to Stampfl's ideas. For Bannister, training at the Maida Vale track in London, these methods were perfect because they were effective and could be done quickly. As a trainee doctor at nearby St. Mary's Hospital, Bannister only had an hour a day to train. He had to make the most of his time.

The 1952 Olympics in Helsinki didn't go his way. The IOC changed the rules to add an additional qualifying round, something Bannister thought favoured those athletes who trained for endurance over speed. He qualified for the final but all his confidence had gone. In the final he finished fourth, the worst position of all. After this failure Bannister went through a low period. He considered giving up running. Then he decided not only to continue, but to set himself a new target: the four-minute mile.

One of the most well-known methods for setting goals is the so-called SMART method. The idea is that when setting a goal you should ensure it is Specific, Measurable, Achievable, Realistic and Timely. For Bannister the four-minute mile was all those things. It is the perfect example of how to set a goal. And there was the added benefit that his performance was not being influenced by his competitors. Trying to win the Olympic 1500 metres final meant racing other athletes, which meant tactics, mostly beyond his control. The world record for the mile, however, was simply a matter of form, pacing and waiting for the right conditions.

Why didn't Roger Bannister give up after Helsinki? Well, he was committed to his sport, and he was good at it. Two strong reasons. But not the whole story. The critical third reason for him not walking away was that he found a goal that inspired him.

The first step of the reverse engineering process is to set a goal. You don't need to be aiming for world records. It doesn't even need to be SMART (more on that later). You just need the focus and energy to go after it. Bannister had that focus. Find the thing you love and you're already travelling in the right direction.

* * *

I too found the thing I love, though it took a little while. Talk to a professional cyclist and you're likely to find that they've been racing since their early teens, if not before. A local cycling club fosters their talent, educates them in the craft of racing, and in time they progress to more and more professional teams. By the time they turn 21 they could have been racing for a decade. I came to cycling a different way. In Oxford I was just one of the thousands of students who got about by bike. It was six miles from my house to campus, a decent daily round-trip, and I enjoyed the sense of freedom cycling gave me. I'd tried several sports at school – among them football, rugby, squash and tennis – but never quite settled on something that sparked my imagination. At university I joined the athletics club, starting as a 100-metres runner and then moving up through the distances to 800 metres and 1500 metres. I enjoyed running and it was a good outlet for my competitive instincts, but I was never going to trouble the Olympic squad. A friend persuaded me to try triathlons (which comprise a swim, bike ride and run) and I won my first event, the British Universities Super Sprint Championships. The more technical nature of combining three sports seemed to suit me. But in early 2015, during my final year of university, I picked up a foot injury that would have required me to take at least six months off running and triathlons, so instead I simply switched to cycle racing.

Because I was relatively new to the sport I felt I had to try everything – road racing (massed start races on the open road), road time trials (in which cyclists ride alone against the clock) and track. I had found my passion, but I was yet to discover my niche within it. Road racing is the core of the sport – colourful, frenetic and tough. Every young rider dreams of winning the Tour de France. Throwing yourself into a local race around some quiet country lanes on a Sunday morning is the way to begin that long career path. I was fairly good at road racing, earning enough results to move up through the rider categories, which in turn attracted the attention of better racing teams. Road racing was fun but it was riding against the clock that piqued my interest.

Britain has a long heritage of time trialling. In part this is because cycle racing of all kinds was banned on public roads during the 1950s. To get their dose of competition, and pain, cycling clubs organised clandestine time-trial events. At dawn, wearing head-to-toe black like pedalling ninjas, they travelled to secret locations, usually an anonymous lay-by on a main road. Courses had code names, such as F11/10, which are still used today. When racing was legalised these time trials continued much as they had done previously, and have been a mainstay of the British club racing scene ever since. They're a strong proving ground for anyone who wants the very different type of racing that is riding solo against the clock. Chris Boardman's early career, before Olympic and Tour de France glory, was spent smashing up and down dual carriageways with HGVs hurtling past.

To win a road race you need good physiology plus good tactics. In time trialling you need good physiology plus good aerodynamics. In a road race you have to react to your competitors, adapt your strategy on the move. In time trials everything is within the rider's control (apart from the weather), and everything can be planned. I loved the idea that in a time trial all those hours of training and preparation are condensed into one short, intense performance. It's instinctive; for 20 minutes you think about nothing other than the physical effort of making the bike go faster. Cathartic too; whatever is going on in your life you can pour that emotion into the pain in your legs.

At university, as my passion for cycling took hold, I began to see links between my studies and bike racing. My degree was in motor-sport engineering. I'd always enjoyed maths and science and this was a subject that combined them with sport. We studied vehicle dynamics and lap-time simulation, and there was a strong empha-sis on aerodynamics. The penultimate year of my degree was spent on a placement at the Mercedes AMG Petronas F1 team headquar-ters, working on improving the aerodynamics of their car, and while a Formula One car is a very long way from a bike in its complexity, the same principles applied. I learnt a great deal during that year in Formula One. And it wasn't just about wind-tunnel testing; I also learnt about teamwork, problem-solving and the importance of applying intellectual rigour to your work.

Track racing was only at the periphery of my world. In the spring of 2015 my university cycling club friends and I often travelled to Reading to join regular training sessions on the outdoor velodrome at Palmer Park. These were good hard workouts but riding on a tarmac outdoor track is very different to the wooden indoor velodromes where all the serious track racing takes place. Wind plays a factor, as it does in road races, the surface is lumpy, and the track is much longer and therefore less banked. Still, it was there at Palmer Park that I first began to measure metrics such as CdA – a mathematical expression of how aerodynamic you are – and look for opportunities to improve the way I was riding through the air. Being on an outdoor velodrome made the data unpredictable but I was excited by the potential to study it and improve. I relish the challenge of an intellectual problem, the way it pulls you in and continues to reward you as you dissect and understand it. I love spreadsheets full of data. They always tell a story and they always provide insight, if you look hard enough. What can I say, I'm a geek...

* * *

The history of track racing is as long as the history of the bicycle itself. In the 1870s, as bicycle design developed to include gears and pneumatic tyres, bicycle racing became hugely popular in the United States. Racing moved from flat cinder tracks to wooden velodromes where entrepreneurs could create a more theatrical atmosphere and pack more paying spectators in. Professional racing grew in Europe too, with six-day races (in which pairs of riders raced continuously for six days and six nights) particularly popular.

Despite the rise of road racing, track racing remained popular in the first half of the twentieth century. Most famous road racers served an apprenticeship on the boards of their local velodrome, learning tactics, how to pedal fast and how to handle their bike. And many continued to appear in track meets long after they became famous, usually for a hefty fee.

Since 1896 track racing has featured in the Olympics, and the Olympic cycle dictates much of the investment and preparation each nation puts into the sport. Most national governing bodies, like British Cycling, are funded centrally and the level of that funding is directly linked to Olympic medals. Fewer medals equals budget cuts. Annually the most important events are the World Championships, held in late February, and the World Cup, a series of six events held between September and January.

There are essentially two types of event in track racing – sprints and endurance. The sprint races are short and intense, varying from the head-to-head sprints in which musclebound warriors like Chris Hoy wind up their speed to hurtle around the track for a lap and a half, to the chaotic and dangerous keirin, a bizarre race in which a group of riders follow the pace set by an adapted motorbike called a derny, then sprint like crazy when the derny pulls off the track. These events were too gladiatorial for me. And they didn't suit me physiologically either. I am a skinny endurance athlete, not a powerful sprinter.

The track endurance events have more crossover to road racing and time trials. Bradley Wiggins and Mark Cavendish, to name just two, have been successful in track endurance events. Before his *annus mirabilis* in 2012, Wiggins had already won 10 World Championship medals and five Olympic medals on the track. There are massed start events, such as the points race and the scratch race, but it is the pursuit events that I specialise in. I knew these suited me because of their similarity to time trialling. In the individual pursuit, two riders start on opposite sides of the track. They race – or pursue – each other for four kilometres. The theoretical objective is to catch your opponent, though this only happens if there is a significant mismatch in ability. If the catch is made, the race is over. If not, the fastest person to finish the four kilometres is the winner. Women race over three kilometres; the difference in distance has no logic to it. It is just one of many anachronisms in the way cycling fails to deal with gender equality.

The team pursuit events are the same distances and principle as the individual pursuit, but with four men or women on each team. The objective is to work as a team to beat your opponents and your time is taken on the third man or woman to cross the line.

I love the pursuit events for their simplicity and elegance. Done well, a team pursuit looks effortless, almost automated. It is an event where precision pays off. If you can achieve the perfect synthesis of man and machine you can win the individual pursuit.

Choreograph four men to go fast together and you might just win a team pursuit. And it is an event in which detailed planning always yields results; in the team pursuit if you analyse and plan effectively you can be confident of a good result. At that stage of my life I wanted something that I could plan meticulously to achieve, something that would reward a detailed approach. I felt here was an event in which I could make my mark, perhaps achieve something far beyond my results to date. But if I was going to achieve that, first I needed to put together a team.

* * *

In September 2015, just six months after I had decided to focus solely on cycling, I finished seventh in the individual pursuit at the National Track Championships in Manchester. I had borrowed a track bike and only ridden on a velodrome a handful of times. Considering such haphazard preparation I was pleased with the result. Something lodged in my mind, an inkling that I should start to take track racing seriously. The pursuit was an interesting combination of athleticism and science. There was very little contingency or luck involved. What you put in, you got out – unlike road racing in which you could be phenomenally strong but be beaten by the tactics of others, or just sheer bad luck. The importance of aerodynamics in the pursuit was relevant to my studies and my experience at Mercedes AMG Petronas and I felt I could bring some new thinking to the event. In terms of a career in bike racing, track was a disastrous idea; there is no money in track racing. But if you follow the money, you will only ever follow the way things have always been done. From my experiences in sport I have found that innovation has to come from passion first, and with perseverance, success and money will follow. So throughout the summer of 2016 I was thinking about how to have a serious crack at the next National Track Championships. After the 2015 championships in which I finished seventh, British Cycling moved the event to January to better fit in with the international calendar for track racing, so no championships were held in 2016 – the next ones would be in January 2017. This felt like a stroke of luck because it gave me extra time to prepare, yet I knew those few months would flash by. One of my team-mates during that road season was Charlie Tanfield. Though only 20 at the time, Charlie's potential was clear to everyone around him. He was stylish on the bike, despite his tall frame, and very fast. And Charlie was hungry to prove himself. He was from a cycling family from North Yorkshire. His older brother Harry was also a professional cyclist and in 2016 Harry was seeing considerable success on the road. The brothers were born on the same day two years apart. They are as close as they are competitive.

During the summer of 2016 Charlie and I spent a lot of time together. Bike races are an intense experience but surrounded by long periods of boredom in which you can plan for the future. Many hours are spent on long training rides, car journeys to races and hanging about in airport lounges. Charlie and I discussed the idea of us both riding the individual pursuit. What would it take to win the national championship? How much preparation would we need to be in with a realistic chance of winning? Then the subject of the team pursuit came up. Since well before either of us could remember, the team pursuit at the National Championships had been dominated by the British Cycling Academy teams. These were squads working towards a level where they might represent Great Britain at the Olympics and World Championships. British Cycling rarely put their top-flight Great Britain riders into the National Championships, deeming it an event slightly below these gods of the track, just as they didn't bring out their fastest, most secret equipment for fear that images of it might get into the hands of rival nations. Nevertheless, winning the pursuit events was a point of pride for British Cycling and they took them seriously enough, sending the riders they felt sure would win comfortably. No amateur team had ever entered the team pursuit with a focused approach, so British Cycling had never been challenged. But we were not going to challenge anyone with only two riders.

Finding a third was straightforward. We knew Jonny Wale from training sessions at Derby velodrome and from university time-trial competitions. Jonny specialised in the kilometre, a track time trial that bridges the gap between the sprint and endurance events – a simple but phenomenally tough event. From a standing start the rider has to use immense power to get up to full speed as quickly as possible, then maintain it for the rest of the distance. Jonny was one of the more exuberant characters at the velodrome, always ready with a wisecrack. Whenever I spoke to him I could sense that he was very perceptive, and his mind was always moving quickly, usually looking for the next killer piece of banter.

As a kilometre rider he was physically just as fast, and most importantly he was keen to get involved. I could see that beneath the joker exterior lay an athlete who was committed to his sport.

Before dedicating himself to cycling, Jonny had also been a chef in an exclusive restaurant, and I felt that this would surely have some added benefits for the team.

In late September Charlie was riding the Tour of Poyang Lake stage race in China. Held over 11 days, the race had a reputation for being lucrative for European riders. The organisers paid for all expenses, including flights, and the prize money was attractive. Riding alongside Charlie was Jacob Tipper, a rider I knew from the domestic road and time-trial scene. Tipper – as everyone calls him – was a strong sprinter whose focus was on road racing. He was equally able in time trials, and what interested me too was his background in sports science. As a sideline he coached other riders and was known for his blend of pragmatism and science. I had a feeling he would make the perfect fourth man for our team, but I knew persuading him to join us was not going to be easy. Tipper is as pessimistic as I am optimistic. We are natural counterparts and while that makes for a neat balance, it can also bring many frustrating conversations. Even before I put forward my idea, Tipper already thought I was crazy.

Somewhere in the Jiangxi province, Tipper was sitting next to Charlie on a bus when I WhatsApped him. Did he fancy having a crack at the team pursuit National Championships in January? We needed a fourth man. All he would have to do is ride four or five laps on the front then peel off and head for the showers.

Tipper said no.

You wouldn't even need to do any extra training, I said. And we're thinking of expanding our road team for the following year so you'd be part of that too (I knew he was not very happy in his current team).

Tipper said maybe.

Eventually, after a long chain of messages, he said yes. Of the journey we were setting out on, this became one of the first lessons to live by: perseverance. Tipper was on board, though was clearly sceptical.

Still, we had our squad. In five weeks we'd be racing for a medal in the four-kilometre team pursuit at the National Track Championships in Manchester. Next, we had to work out how we were going to achieve our goal.

A month of hard training lay ahead of us. But I knew that alone would not be enough. We had to understand precisely what it would take to get that medal. We had to start at the end.

2

Commit to a goal

Let us return to that cool May evening in 1954. Roger Bannister breaks the four-minute barrier for the mile and is immortalised. This was a simple, finite goal. Part of the reason that the record became so iconic, so sought after, was that athletes had been chasing it for over 50 years. It had seemed tantalisingly close, but somehow had eluded the best legs – and minds – in distance running. When Bannister took to the track, the world record stood at 4 minutes, 1.3 seconds, set by Sweden's Gunder Hägg in 1945. It took nine years to find 1.3 seconds' worth of extra speed.

What held all those world-class athletes back? It was not a lack of physical ability. Journalist and runner John Bryant wrote, "For years milers had been striving against the clock, but the elusive four minutes had always beaten them," he notes. "It had become as much a psychological barrier as a physical one. And like an unconquerable mountain, the closer it was approached, the more daunting it seemed."

The athletes doubted not only their own ability, but whether it could be done at all. The feat seemed impossible. Beyond the limit of human endurance. The running community hypothesised that if the record were to be broken, it would only happen under perfect conditions – a warm day with little wind, a fast clay track (runners at the time believed that Scandinavian tracks were the quickest) with a huge crowd to cheer the runners on. Yet when Bannister did achieve the impossible it was under far from perfect conditions – the track was made of cinders, it was cold and blustery, and the crowd was small.

For those athletes who had been aiming to break through the four-minute barrier, when Bannister did so, their focus had to shift. Their goal was gone. So they set new goals, and for most it was simply breaking the world record, whatever figure that meant. And I believe that seemed to be much easier, psychologically, because the emphasis was more on beating a fellow human being, not the clock. Less than two months later, an Australian, John Landy, beat Bannister's new record, running 3 minutes, 58 seconds. A year later three athletes went under four minutes in a single race. And by 1958, the record had been chopped to 3 minutes, 54 seconds. Having taken nearly a decade to find 1.3 seconds, the elite running world found six seconds in four years.

The point here is that progression does not always come smoothly. Once the mental barrier was gone, several athletes were able to go under four minutes for the mile. They saw that it was not impossible and that freed them up to attack it. Indeed, when we think about it more dispassionately, we can see that four minutes is a kind of arbitrary figure. Since competitive running started, a committed, well-trained athlete could run a mile at a certain pace, and that pace then gave people a time somewhere around four minutes. So, at a certain point of history, breaking that neat round figure was going to become a focus. In itself, four minutes means nothing.

As I write this, in the summer of 2020, the four-kilometre individual pursuit world record stands at 4:01.934, set by the Italian Filippo Ganna in Berlin in February 2020. The progression of this world record has been just as erratic as the mile. In 1996 Chris Boardman recorded 4:11.114 and it took 15 years for someone to beat that time. It then took another seven years for the record to come down to 4:07.251.

Twenty-five years ago the prospect of someone riding four kilometres in under four minutes (bear in mind that's an average speed of 60 kilometres per hour) seemed unimaginable. Now it is just a matter of time, and there is very little media buzz about it. Why? Because everyone involved in the world of elite pursuit events accepts that it is theoretically possible. It is inevitable. In pursuiting, four minutes has not become a mental barrier because people have come to understand that any record can be broken. It just takes time, a clear plan and hard work.

For Jonny, Tipper, Charlie and I, our naivety meant we had not built up any mental barriers about what we were taking on. We had nothing to lose when we set out to get a medal at the National Championships. Plus, we didn't really have time to think about it.

* * *

Opened in March 2015, Derby Arena is an impressive multi-sports facility on the south-east edge of the city. The building is an undulating oval shape, composed of gold and silver tiles that glisten in the sun. As you approach the arena's front entrance there is a long, slim curving window. Standing out above it are two darker rectangles. Together these three features give the impression of a face, though whether the mouth is smiling or gripped by the pain of cycling on a velodrome is open to interpretation.

The arena facilitates training and competition for badminton, and has hosted many entertainment and corporate events, but its heart is the velodrome. Unlike the velodromes of London, Berlin, Minsk and others, Derby velodrome was built to be a regional hub rather than to host international events. There were regular training sessions for local clubs, lessons in riding on the track to encourage newcomers to the sport, and a Tuesday night race league. Like all good velodromes, the track was constructed from Siberian pine. Laid end to end the planks would stretch for 40 kilometres, and 265,000 nails were hand-driven to keep those planks down.

For the four of us, Derby was the perfect training facility. We could get easy access to the track, there was a gym on site, and the café was pretty good too. Sometimes, on a quiet Tuesday morning in the depths of winter, it felt as though we had the place to ourselves.

The first training session there, in December 2016, didn't get off to a good start, as Tipper turned up late and with a hangover from a mate's stag do. Still, he got through the session without crashing or vomiting. We started to run through the basics of how to ride a team pursuit. None of us had any experience in the discipline, but the fundamentals will make sense to any cyclist.

The objective is to ride as a team over four kilometres, or 16 laps, with the finishing time taken on the front wheel of the third man. In any form of cycling (apart from time trials where you ride alone), drafting is critically important. In road racing, for example, it defines the pattern of every race; it is why racers ride in one big pack, choosing very carefully the moment to strike out for the finish line. The principle is that riding close behind another rider saves about 30 to 50 per cent energy because the rider in front is doing more work to break into the wind. The faster you are travelling, and the stronger the wind, the more energy you save. So road racing becomes a game of trying to conserve energy by staying out of the wind. Attacking alone in the first kilometre is pointless. Saving your energy then attacking in the last kilometre is a much better plan.

On the track the effect of drafting is even more pronounced. In the team pursuit four riders work together. The first rider breaks through undisturbed air. This creates a wake of disturbed air, effectively creating a lower air speed for each rider behind. The benefit to the riders in second, third and fourth positions increases as you go down the line and can be as high as 70 per cent for the fourth man. So while the rider on the front is pedalling at close to his maximum energy levels, the rider at the back is (relatively) just cruising.

From a standing start, the team sprint to get up to top speed as quickly as possible, then settle into a line. The order is planned. The first man has to work the hardest to get into his position. From then the idea is for the four riders to ride in a tidy, compact line.

Each rider's front wheel should be as close as possible to the rear wheel of the rider in front, just a handful of centimetres. When you are riding at close to 60 kilometres per hour this is no mean feat. Track bikes have no brakes, and we use extended handlebars that allow us to stretch forward over the bike – great for aerodynamic efficiency but not so good at handling sudden changes in speed or direction. So when you are riding in the line you are constantly making tiny adjustments to the position of your front wheel. With a little experience you do this instinctively. Get it wrong and you will touch the wheel in front. Not long after you'll be flying through the air towards the track. And crashing on a wooden track tends to give you pretty nasty splinters in all kinds of sensitive places. To spread the workload efficiently across the team, pursuit teams change positions regularly. When it is time for a change, the rider on the front uses one of the steep banking sections at either end of the track, swings up the banking and lets the other three riders pass beneath him, then drops down to the back of the line. It may look as if that rider is having a bit of a breather as he swings up. Not so. Executing a smooth change is over in the blink of an eye and it is pretty stressful – you have to drop down to slot in close behind the third rider. Allow a gap to open and you're back to breaking the air yourself, only now off the back of the group. In this scenario, even if you can close that gap, you will have wasted a lot of energy doing so and when you get back on the front you will suffer.

A well-drilled pursuit team is a beautiful thing to watch. The four riders ride so closely that they seem to be part of one organism. Changes are fluid and smooth. The pace is consistent. Traditional orthodoxy is that the four should be physically well matched, both in their capacity for power output and their physique. National teams can achieve this because they are selecting from a gene pool of thousands. Some teams are so well matched that when riding in their national team skinsuits and aero helmets, it is impossible to tell the four men apart. Not us – in the velodrome in Derby, we looked like the bunch of misfits we were.

During the first week of training it soon became apparent how diverse we were as riders. Charlie and I were similar in our endurance, our naturally aerodynamic position on the bike and our ragged changes. We could go fast, but lost time on every change. Jonny, being a kilo rider, had immense power over a shorter distance. And Tipper just couldn't keep up, even without a hangover.

So we could get a decent two- or three-hour session on the track, our slots often started eye-wateringly early. I found it a struggle to get out of bed before dawn, force some porridge down my neck and bundle all my kit into the car. I loaded myself up with my bike, kit bag, laptop bag, spare wheels, pump and anything else I could carry, then having struggled to lock my car, headed inside. (At the velodrome I always parked as close as possible to the door, to avoid being out in the cold too long.) Going from the gloom of a winter's morning to the harsh fluorescent lights of the velodrome was a blast to the synapses. Another – equally unwelcome – was the pumping dance music that seemed to be playing on a continual loop day and night.

Settled on folding chairs in the track centre, amid white badminton court nets, we drank coffee and grunted at each other. I fired up my laptop, wheels were changed, cycling shoes pulled on, muscles stretched, jokes exchanged and soon enough we each started doing a warm-up on a set of rollers – three stationary rolling drums that you place your bike on and pedal, going nowhere no matter how fast you pedal. In every training session it was Jonny who was the motivating force. He cajoled us to keep putting in the time on the track, to stop messing about, to take things seriously. Right from the start it was clear just how much this project meant to him.

Whenever we came to the track we were loud and pretty chaotic. Partly to drown out the awful music played over the arena's speakers, we brought our own speaker and played raucous rock music. 'Gay Bar' by Electric Six was a favourite. Unfortunately our performances didn't quite live up to our attitude; the local cycling teams there with us in the track centre watched with wry smiles as we failed over and over again to stick together over the four kilometres. Yet some saw our potential. In particular, a young woman called Ellie Green who was there helping a team sponsored by her father's bike shop, Langdale Lightweights. Ellie found us hilarious, but could also see our ambition and agreed to help us prepare for the National Championships.

By the end of that first week, despite all the chaos, we had recorded a best time of 4:25 for the four-kilometre pursuit, although Tipper usually dropped off with around three laps to go, unable to hold on to Charlie and I, so technically we had not finished the event with three riders. If we replicated that at the National Championships we were in trouble. Whilst the time was about 20 seconds slower than it needed to be for us to get a medal, we had at least made it through those early practice sessions without crashing, and we had learnt a great deal about one another.

Aside from the apparent disparity in our physical capabilities, we all had the same mindset. We all wanted to be there and had committed to pursuing this goal. This is where the relative brevity of the plan worked to its advantage. All four of us could fully commit to it because it was only for four weeks, and those four weeks happened to fall in the quietest time of year for road cycling. We had nothing better to do, and racing inside a warm velodrome was more attractive than putting in hundreds of miles of training on the cold, wet roads of Staffordshire.

There is a theory about goal-setting called 'goal competition'. This holds that one of the biggest obstacles to achieving our goals is our other goals. We tend to have multiple goals at any one time and dividing our energy between them means we're less likely to achieve any of them. The billionaire investor Warren Buffett came up with a rule called 25:5, which underlines this idea. Buffett's personal pilot was a man called Mike Flint, an accomplished professional who had previously flown four US presidents. The two men were discussing Flint's career objectives. Buffett asked Flint to take some time and write down his 25 career objectives. Flint duly came back to his boss with his list of objectives, and Buffett then asked Flint to pick out his top five objectives. Flint now had two lists – his top five objectives, and 20 other objectives. It was clear that Flint was to begin working on his top five immediately. Buffett asked him about the remaining 20 – what did Flint propose to do with those? Flint replied that while they were not his immediate focus, those 20 objectives were still important to him and he would make sure to create time to work on them. No, said Buffett – that list of 20 objectives becomes your list of 20 things to avoid at all costs. Until, that is, you have achieved your list of five. Those things get no attention whatsoever until you have succeeded in your top priorities.

This is effectively what the four of us did during those winter months in Derby. Nothing else mattered. We could commit to this single goal and push everything else aside. What did we have to lose? At the very least, we would learn something about ourselves.

3

Find out what motivates you

Our reasons for taking up the challenge may have been different, but all four of us had something to prove.

Because I had come into the sport relatively late and through an unconventional route, I had missed out on the opportunity to join British Cycling's academy system. Everyone knew that unless you were part of that system you had no hope of turning professional or going to the Olympics. I was ambitious and intensely competitive. I wanted to see how far I could go in the sport. I wanted to make my mark. After years of trying different sports, I had finally found the one I loved and I was not going to let the system beat me.

Charlie's experience of cycling had been very different to mine. He was from a cycling family and had raced since he was 12 years old. At 15 he was recruited to the British Cycling Talent Team, the first stage of their development programme, and seemed set for a progression towards a professional career. Then, a year later, despite achieving good race results, British Cycling dropped him from the programme. The explanation they gave was that he was not behaving like a good athlete. He was not easy to work with and his punctuality was erratic. Devastated, Charlie set about finding an alternative route to achieve his ambitions. He had invested too much in cycling to give up.

The Tanfield personality soon became a running joke among the four of us. Charlie shares with his older brother Harry a laid-back demeanour, with a kind of sleepy good humour and a wry smile. He gets easily distracted and often has several crazy projects on the go, such as making his own carbon fibre cycling shoes in the garden shed. He was notorious for arriving at races late, often apparently oblivious to time ticking away, and perhaps the British Cycling coaches mistook this kind of flaky behaviour for a lack of commitment. Not so. Underneath, Charlie is sharply intelligent and just as ambitious as the rest of us. Being dropped from the British Cycling programme had knocked his confidence; our team became his way to build it up again.

Tipper also came from a traditional cycling background. He had spent his teenage years learning to ride and race with his local club, Halesowen Athletic and Cycling Club, which had a heritage of track racing (their patron is former World Pursuit champion Hugh Porter). British cycling clubs offer a safe and friendly way for young riders to learn and develop. For Tipper the experience inculcated a deep love of the sport in him.

In those years he struggled to make an impact. In the national road racing events that British Cycling watch to find new talent, he often finished at the back of the pack. In the Junior National Pursuit Championships he finished second last. He was a long way off the standard required to get on to the British Cycling programmes. As in many other sports, when aspiring cyclists get to their later teenage years, there is often a decision point. The transition to university or the world of work can prompt young athletes to give up their hopes of sporting success. An influx of new people, new environments and new demands on their time just make it seem too hard to keep putting in the training hours. Tipper, however, was driven to keep going, in part simply because he enjoyed racing so much.

In the senior ranks he found a niche as a road sprinter – the kind of speedy rider that excels in the final 200 metres of a race – and as a short distance time triallist. When we met he was riding at the same level of domestic racing as I was, with little expectation of progressing to world-class racing. His motivation for joining us was simple: a National Championships medal. For Tipper, to be British champion was a goal that, if achieved, could be the highlight of his career. At the time, it seemed to him that this might be his only opportunity to get one.

Because we were outside the system, we had the freedom to do whatever we thought would help us go faster. We could play to our strengths. A good example is Tipper's pedalling style. Part of the reason Tipper had struggled at national level as a junior was that, as with some bigger riders, his physiology favoured pedalling a bigger gear, meaning his optimal cadence was lower than most. British Cycling coaches took the view that a higher cadence on a lower gear was better for everyone, and they pushed this idea at every level, from the elite Olympic squads all the way down to the children in cycling clubs. For children there is a good argument to spin the pedals fast (it saves too much pressure being applied to growing joints), so turning the ship in individual instances would become too much of an institutional and logistical nightmare. However, our freedom as a team allowed us to assess that the policy of high cadence should not have been applied to a six-foot 18-year-old, and certainly wouldn't apply to Tipper now. So we were able to change it up. Tipper felt happier pedalling slower – by using bigger gears he was going faster with lower perceived exertion – and there was nothing intrinsically wrong with it. Some of the old hands who saw us training at Derby Arena (and were always quick to offer their advice) argued that his start would be compromised. It wasn't, because Tipper can produce the required power to get up to full speed at a much lower cadence than the rest of us. Yet because British Cycling had the orthodoxy of low gears and high cadence, and because Tipper understandably wanted to be noticed and brought into an academy programme, he had tried to change his natural pedalling style. Not surprisingly, it did not work.

When the four of us came together, Jonny and I were 25, Charlie was 20 and Tipper was 24. Yet somehow Tipper seemed the oldest and most experienced. After all, he had over a decade of racing experience behind him and had got to where he was on his own. Having forged his own path so far, he was sceptical about relinquishing control of his destiny to others. He could be dour and difficult, but once he committed to the objective he put everything into it.

Jonny's ambition in cycling was very different to the rest of us. All his adult life he has suffered from bipolar disorder. Depression has taken him to some very dark places and he lives with it every day. Before we met him, psychologists told him that elite sport was not a good place for someone with bipolar disorder – that the pressure and the roller-coaster emotion would be too much. But Jonny knows himself. Cycling is his happy place. It is good for him, even taking into account all its ups and downs.

When he started cycling seriously, in university, he wasn't bothered about racing. He just loved the training, going out and bashing out big sessions on the bike. When I met Jonny and we began discussing the team pursuit, he was trying to find a way out of a low period. Becoming part of the team was a form of rehabilitation. We needed him, and he was valued. He felt he could prove his self-worth to himself if he performed well during training. For Jonny that was enough. He had no particular ambition to be British champion or any other racing goal.

Like Tipper, though for different reasons, Jonny has had to become resilient and self-sufficient. Jonny believes that you have to accept who you are, understand the cards you've been dealt and manage them the best you can. Cycling has become his way of, as he puts it, leaving a mark on life. On his bad days he is prone to look at other people's lives and think that they are perfect, that everyone else is achieving something, and that his own life is empty and meaningless. Riding bike races, and the work that goes into preparing for them, gives him hope. I feel privileged to have worked alongside Jonny and gained just a little insight into what makes him tick. It has been a powerful learning experience to get this perspective on sport.

So we all committed to the goal of winning a medal at national level. And though our underlying motivations may have been different, they all amounted to the same thing. We wanted to prove ourselves to the cycling world. We wanted to show that we were capable of taking on riders produced by the system that had ignored or rejected us.

It can be useful to understand why you want something. But not essential. You could argue that Charlie wanted to exact some kind of revenge on British Cycling for dropping him from their programme. That he wanted to show them they were wrong. Or that he wanted to get one over on his big brother. Perhaps those were his motivations. It doesn't really matter. Understanding his own motivation, or not, made no difference to how fast Charlie could ride his bike.

Set a goal and work towards it with all the commitment and resources you can muster. Trust your instincts. Once you have achieved your goal there will be time and space to look back and analyse yourself. Until then, the only thing that matters is forward momentum.

* * *

In the weeks leading up to the National Championships, at the start of January 2017, we were training at Derby Arena four or five times a week. And because most of our sessions started at six in the morning, we knew we had to all base ourselves as close as possible to the track. That way, we could still get a half-decent night's sleep. Staying in hotels was not an option, so Jonny suggested the next best thing. Well, you can always crash on my floor, he shrugged. A generous offer, though Jonny was living in the University of Loughborough halls of residence at the time, so having the three of us sleep on his floor was somewhat tricky. Our solution was that we made a camp on the floor of the communal kitchen nearest to Jonny's room. We did get quite a lot of bemused looks from the other students but they seemed to accept our presence without rancour. One of the drawbacks of sleeping in a university kitchen was that every time a student got up to use the toilet – or came back from a party in the small hours of the morning – they would set off the automatic sensors, and all the lights in the communal areas would come on.

At that time our training was pretty limited in scope. Naively, we believed that to win a four-kilometre track race, the best way to prepare was by riding four-kilometre track races, over and over again. The only variation in our sessions was that sometimes we did dead starts, as the races would feature, and other times we did flying starts, in which we were already up to full speed when the clock started. If anyone had asked us to explain why we did the latter, we would not have had a very good explanation. Still, it got us used to riding together as a unit and by the new year we were feeling more confident that we would not embarrass ourselves at the upcoming races.

A week before the National Championships in Manchester we travelled to Wales for our first competitive outing as a team. The event was the Welsh Championships, which was run as an open event, meaning any team in the UK could enter. In a strange turn of fate we were drawn to race in the qualifying round against Lang-dale Lightweights, the team with whom we shared Derby Arena for training. Our main objective was simply to finish with three men. I wanted to try to go for a fast time, but I had to keep reminding myself that this was just a dress rehearsal. Going fast meant nothing if we could not hold the team together to the line.

We got away from the start line cleanly and sprinted down the back straight to get up to full speed before settling into formation. I did the first turn on the front, then swung off to let Jonny come through. The pre-race nerves now transformed into adrenaline. Jonny pushed the pace hard over the next four laps, which passed in a blur. It was exhilarating to finally be racing with my friends, to begin the realisation of our ambitions. I could see nothing other than the rider in front of me and yet I was also aware in my peripheral vision of the crowd and the officials and the clock by the trackside, as well as being able to hear the announcer calling out our names.

Jonny swung off as planned after a five-lap turn, leaving Charlie to come through to the front. Now we were in the same straight as our opponents. We were going to catch them. Charlie kept the pace steady, knowing that the race was already effectively won. I was on his wheel. We drew closer and closer, then, when we were only two metres behind them, their fourth man touched his front wheel on to the back wheel of their third man. Both of them went crashing down on to the track. Charlie and I had nowhere to go and smashed into them, then into the banking of the track. Tipper, who'd been sitting at the back of our line, managed to flick his bike up the banking to avoid the tangle of bikes and bodies in front of him. As

Charlie and I gracelessly slid down the boards, accumulating some nasty burns as we went, Tipper rode on, shouting at the two, somewhat stunned, remaining riders of Langdale Lightweights. "You've fucked it! You've proper fucked it!" he shouted.

Shaken, bruised and angry, we drove home from Wales to begin our final preparations for the National Championships. It had not been an auspicious start to our team's journey.

4

Understand the competition

We didn't really expect to beat the British Cycling Academy team. It was just too outrageous. How could the four of us come together only five weeks before the event, with no experience, no coach, no budget, and expect to beat the reigning champions? They had years of coaching experience on their side, equipment developed by a specialist research team and that extensive gene pool. I knew Tipper, Jonny and Charlie were simply aiming to get on the podium, though. Getting a medal was a reasonable, if stretching, aim, when you considered where we were as individual riders. And for any rider, getting a medal at your National Championships was a big deal.

By this time, the other three had come to know me for my wild optimism. It is still often the basis for a joke at my expense. Perhaps it is a way of kidding myself into trying things, or keeping going when it feels tough, but it can be a useful tool. Expect more of your-self. Set daunting goals. You might just get close to them. During those four weeks I didn't say much, but I was excited about the prospect of taking on British Cycling. I wasn't sure that we could beat them, but I did think we could get to the finals and give them a close run. Why?

Complacency. For more than a decade British Cycling had dominated the team pursuit at the National Championships. There was no credible competition for them, so competitions like these had become glorified training exercises. They used this event to test their riders, try out different combinations of riders, and they rarely used their fastest equipment as they saved that for international events. They approached the Championships with the assumption that they were going to win, and that is always dangerous. One of our key advantages was the element of surprise. If they didn't know how serious we were, perhaps we could blindside them.

One of my earliest memories of seeing cycling on the television was Bradley Wiggins winning the individual pursuit at the 2004 Athens Olympics. Though there had been Olympic medals before 2004 – most notably Jason Queally's surprise gold in the kilo in Sydney four years earlier and Chris Boardman's rather less surprising gold in the individual pursuit in Barcelona in 1992 – the Athens Games were the first in which Great Britain looked like a serious player on the world stage.

British Cycling was formed in 1959 and is the official governing body for the sport in Great Britain. It is recognised by the sport's international governing body, the Union Cycliste Internationale (UCI), and selects the teams that represent Great Britain internationally. All cycle sport in Great Britain has to be registered through

British Cycling. The organisation is based in offices adjoining the Manchester velodrome, just across the road from Manchester City's stadium. Come to race in Manchester and you are very much on British Cycling's home turf.

Until the late nineties British Cycling was a shoestring operation with a handful of full-time staff and a meagre budget. The sport was effectively run by an army of volunteers, and if a young rider wanted to progress to the highest levels of racing, he or she knew they had to turn professional as quickly as possible. That usually meant moving to France or Belgium where a sound income (for men, anyway) could be secured with a commercially sponsored road team, learning French and learning to ride in tough Continental races. Accordingly British success was sporadic and when it happened, it happened principally on the road, where the money was. The idea that British Cycling helped any of the riders from this era would have been laughable.

The moment when change began came in November 1996 in, of all places, the House of Commons. Labour MP Jon Trickett stood up and questioned whether the British Cycling Federation (as it was called then) was fit for purpose. He went on to accuse the organisation of a lack of vision and leadership, of wasting its taxpayer funding. The Sports Council, which soon after transformed into UK Sport, began an audit of British Cycling and uncovered a fragile financial position, shoddy accounting practices and conflicts of interest among the members of the board. But Trickett and UK Sport were late to the party. Even before Trickett made his speech in the House of Commons, the entire BCF board had been removed at the 1996 AGM, voted out by cycling club delegates. A new generation of leaders came to the fore, and they had a much grander vision for British cycle sport.

In 1997 Peter Keen was appointed British Cycling's first ever Head of Performance. Keen had been the national track cycling coach and, perhaps more importantly, he was Chris Boardman's coach. Having steered Boardman to Olympic and World Championship success, then into European road racing (Boardman won the opening time trial of the Tour de France three times), and with an academic background in exercise physiology, Keen had both the experience and the modern thinking needed to revitalise British Cycling. His vision crystallised into the World Class Performance Plan (WCPP). Supported by long-term funding from UK Sport, Keen was able to pay a salary to his elite riders and invest in a new coaching team.

Over the following years he was joined by Dave Brailsford, Shane Sutton, Rod Ellingworth and others, and the WCPP became a blueprint for success. Between them, the team of coaches around Keen had a blend of racing experience, sports science and management skills. It proved to be an effective alchemy; a group of talented and driven coaches whose skill sets complemented one another. Their goal was simple and clear – Olympic gold medals. The focus was on track racing, to the exclusion of all other racing disciplines. This was because that was Keen's background, but it was also partly down to the fact that success in track racing was more controllable than the contingency and labyrinthine tactics of road racing. And Olympic track medals would mean more funding. When Keen left

British Cycling in 2004, he had transformed the elite performance aspect of British Cycling and set the direction for future success. That Keen did not stick around to see that success crystallised into medals was more a reflection of his personality than a judgement on the organisation or the team. He was cerebral and visionary. For Keen, it seems, the exciting bit was writing the plan. The delivery of the plan, which included the more hands-on, often messy business of managing athletes and staff, was less appealing. After leaving British Cycling, Keen moved on to UK Sport, the body responsible for delivering Olympic and Paralympic success across all sports. There he wrote the plans for Britain's hugely successful performance at the 2012 London Olympic Games. In his place at British Cycling, Brailsford, a man much more adept at managing teams, took over at the top.

The 2008 Games in Beijing made household names of Chris Hoy, Victoria Pendleton and Bradley Wiggins and sparked a cycling revolution in Britain. Suddenly everyone wanted to ride their bike. From a sport practised virtually in secret by a minority, cycling was acclaimed as the new golf – better for your health, though with an equally dubious fashion sense. That has benefited everyone involved in the sport at a grassroots level, me included, by bringing bike racing into the public consciousness.

Great Britain's track racing juggernaut rumbled on towards London 2012. Meanwhile Brailsford was feeling confident enough to diversify. In 2008 the global broadcasting corporation Sky, run at the time by cycling fan James Murdoch, signed up to sponsor the Great Britain team. Brailsford pitched to them the idea of a professional road team that would aim to win the Tour de France within five years. Sky said yes, and Team Sky was born. At the time the idea of a British team winning the Tour de France seemed very ambitious, even ludicrous, given how far behind Britain had been as a cycling nation only 10 years earlier. But Brailsford had a plan. In those early years of Sky's involvement, British Cycling and Team Sky became almost indistinguishable. At an operation level there was no clear boundary between them and Brailsford was in charge of both. Team Sky capitalised on all the knowledge and resources at British Cycling. In effect Team Sky was built on the foundations of the WCPP. Peter Keen would later claim that Team Sky had 'asset-stripped' British Cycling.

The success came sooner than anyone expected. Bradley Wiggins landed the team's first Tour de France victory in 2012, and grand tour success has continued ever since, with Chris Froome, Geraint Thomas and Colombian Egan Bernal.

But the success had a cost. By 2016 British Cycling was embroiled in controversy, accused of sexism, bullying and a toxic management culture. There were hints of doping too, connected to Team Sky. A parliamentary select committee instigated an inquiry. Questions were asked in the House of Commons. Twenty years after Trickett had stood up in Parliament and claimed the organisation was not fit for purpose, British Cycling was accused of institutional failure again. This time the accusation was that the drive to win had come at a personal cost to riders and staff. In 2016, there was another change of leadership and a new generation of coaches moved up the ladder to lead the programme.

Yet, despite this new guard, the structural legacy of the WCPP remains even now. Today the system for developing promising riders towards Olympic success is much the same as the one Keen created in the early 2000s. It comprises three stages:

1. **Foundation.** For riders aged 14 to 16, this is where British Cycling begin to invest in individuals and train them for the next stage.

2. **Academy.** This stage is split into two – Junior for riders aged 16 to 18 and Senior for riders aged 18 to 21. In the Junior Academy the riders are coached much more intensively than in Foundation and are taken to international races. The Senior Academy is seen as a finishing school for the racers, preparing them for the top-flight international racing and the final stage of the programme.

3. **Podium Programme.** As British Cycling put it, this is the 'pinnacle of the pathway' for elite riders. Olympic and World Championship medals are expected. Each rider is fully supported and has access to British Cycling's best resources.

To me there's nothing inherently wrong with this structure. It makes sense. It has worked for British Cycling for nearly 20 years, so why change it?

Well, by 2016 that shift was already beginning to take place. Most of the innovative and creative people who delivered success in Beijing and London had left the organisation. The lid had been lifted on the toxic side effects of British Cycling's culture, and the new leadership – rightly – wanted to put in place a framework that would prevent the same kind of rogue behaviour happening again. This meant creating a process for everything. During 2016 I was racing at an elite level in British road races and time trials, a small world in which the same few hundred people see each other every week for a race and a good old gossip. Rumours were circulating that the Great Britain team were getting bogged down in bureaucracy. Innovation was being stifled. I took the rumours with the proverbial pinch of salt, but in time they proved to be true.

One example of this stifling of innovation was that if a coach had an idea for a new method, he would have to get three managers all to approve it in writing. At best this would slow down the testing of the idea. At worst it might put the coach off asking at all. Having the agility to test new ideas quickly is essential to high performance in any sport. Athletes are busy people. They don't want to be kept hanging around while a phalanx of staff have long discussions. The quicker you can test ideas, the quicker you can find those gems that will deliver real performance gains. Give me a rider in a velodrome and I can do 15 aerodynamic tests in less than two hours. In the same time British Cycling might do five tests. The difference is firstly that they have many more people involved, and everyone wants to make a point. And because of the managerial history of British Cycling, theirs is not a rider-centric system. They don't place the rider at the centre of everything they do, which is why they don't care if they keep the rider hanging around at the velodrome, and in doing so losing the goodwill of that rider.

Another legacy of the British Cycling success story, and its subsequent implosion, was the instinct among the organisation's staff to protect their own job and reputation. The Olympic gold medals won in 2008 and 2012 were the products of a team composed of three parts. The riders and coaches were most visible to anyone watching on television, yet behind them was a whole range of what might be called the back-room staff: engineers, physiotherapists, psychologists, masseurs, mechanics, nutritionists and others.

Cycling has always had coaches devoted to understanding and improving their charges' physiology. The forensic-level focus on the engineering aspect was new. Before Beijing a group of people known as the Secret Squirrel Club came together to develop the equipment that the Great Britain team would use – bikes, helmets, clothing, shoes; anything the rider would use in competition. The approach was rigorous and intense. The budget was impressive (leading to complaints from other parts of cycle sport that they had to run their operations on a shoestring because all the body's funding was being pumped into making fast handlebars for the track team). The most famous face of the Secret Squirrel Club was Chris Boardman. Everyone working on the project was smart, educated and brought with them specialist knowledge. Olympic success was built on the combined power of the latest physiological science (in which the coaches were supported by Loughborough University) and the very fast kit produced by the Secret Squirrel Club.

By 2016 the mindset had begun to change. The coaching staff wanted to promote the idea that all the team's success over the years had been down to physiology, and that equipment developments made little or no difference. Plainly wrong. And pretty daft, because it is like saying physics has no impact on a moving object. Newton would be turning in his grave. It is akin to saying that a Formula One car wins or loses on its engine, and aerodynamics makes no difference. Or, that a swimmer wins or loses on strength alone, and the smoothness of their bodies makes no difference. Taking it even further, how would an elite diver gain the height they need from the springboard without using Newton's third law of action and reaction? In any sport, success will only come when *all* the factors affecting performance are understood and optimised. The weightings will vary – for example aerodynamics is clearly more important in cycling than in gymnastics – but there always has to be a balanced approach within the team. Underpinning that must be a culture of giving due respect to the experts in each field.

Whether the Great Britain coaches genuinely believed this, or just wanted to protect their jobs, the effect was that they alienated all the smart people who had been such a key part of the team. The Secret Squirrel Club disbanded. The relationship with Loughborough University came to an end.

British Cycling had stopped working as a team. Complacency, and a degree of arrogance, had crept in. The mindset had moved from one of innovation and creativity, to one of closed-mindedness. Add a tangle of red tape into the mix, and it is not surprising that the Great Britain cycling team was not getting any faster.

Sports science, like all branches of science, is continually moving on. Universities encourage their students to challenge and improve every established idea. Commercial technology companies play a crucial role in this process, providing more and more sophisticated technology to support research, and in turn providing career opportunities for sports science graduates. If Formula One is the apex of this because of its huge resources and because it is so tech-dependent, endurance sports like cycling, running and rowing are subject to a continual tension between tradition and technology. There are still those in cycling who do not understand the physiology of training, the models and knowledge that you need to have as a sound basis on which to train young riders. The problem British Cycling had in 2016 was that they were still favouring training models a decade out of date, and that is a long time in sports science.

By early 2017 I could see an opportunity. Complacency at British Cycling would inevitably mean a plateau in their performance. Any team prepared to keep innovating, to approach the team pursuit and individual pursuit with a fresh pair of eyes, and with the agility to try out new ideas quickly, would reap the rewards. We might have been a bunch of unproven amateurs but I knew our trajectory could be steeply upwards if we worked hard and took nothing for granted.

For example, the usual frequency of changing the lead rider in the team pursuit is once per lap. That is 15 changes per race. That is just the way it has always been done, and it seemed crazy to me. A simple mathematical calculation told me that every change costs the team a tenth of a second – this is just the time lost by the front rider moving to the back of the line. A further consideration is the way changing disrupts the smoothness of the unit. The pace can surge or drop and the aerodynamic profile of the team can become untidy. So why not do fewer changes? If we changed every two laps, we would halve the number of changes and save nearly a second versus the one-lap strategy. This seemed so obvious to me that I could not believe no one had done it before.

It is natural to feel daunted when you take on an opponent or a system that has more power, more resources and more history of success. Just remember that every system has flaws. Every individual has flaws. And by understanding that the competition is flawed, you validate the idea that it can be beaten. Reverse engineering is built on the idea of studying something closely. If a car manufacturer wants to understand how its rival has built their new groundbreaking high-performance electric car, they get hold of as much information as they can about it and pore over that information with a forensic eye. Ideally they would get hold of that new car and take it apart, piece by piece.

That car manufacturer doesn't just want to match precisely what their rival has done. They want to improve it. So they disassemble the car and study it closely, but also keep an open mind to see the possibilities for further development.

Reverse engineering is also widely used in software development, particularly when the developer wishes to add new features to an existing product. It is also commonly employed in software security when a company wants to test the strength of its product's security. Some companies even go as far as employing so-called ethical hackers who will hack into a product – with permission – and see if they can disassemble it.

The interesting thing to note is that there is an underlying assumption in every scenario in which reverse engineering is used – that the product or system can be improved. Whatever the challenge you have set yourself, start from the perspective that its system is flawed.

Faced with a job interview at a multinational company? Remember that its managers will be frustrated by bureaucracy that slows down every decision. Perhaps there is an opportunity for you there.

Lining up against an athlete who has been successful for years? Remember that those who win big tend to stick to the same old methods of preparation, and in time they get complacent. Their success becomes their weakness. Plus, they have to start losing at some point. You could be the one who surprises them.

Setting up a small business and feel like you are making it up as you go along? Remember that the established rival companies in your field went through precisely the same experience. They got things wrong, and *continue* to get things wrong.

Keep breaking things down. Don't look at the competition's performance, look at how they got there. And more importantly, look at how you will get there, by whichever route works for you. Be different, be obtuse, be annoying and, if necessary, be a laughing stock. You know where you are headed. You are only crazy until what you are doing works; then you are a genius. In reverse engineering we dismantle what it is we want to achieve, we understand it, see its imperfections. And this process gives us the confidence to take it on.

5

Find out what to optimise

Socks are very important in pursuit races. They are the equivalent of the wing mirrors on a Formula One car in that they seem only to fulfil a simple function, yet have secret power to alter performance. In both examples, aerodynamics is the secret.

As a rider moves through the air on his bike, his feet are the part of his body that causes the most turbulence. Feet, ankles and calves are not the most naturally aerodynamic things. Add in the buckles, straps, dials or laces on a shoe and you have a lot of different shapes and surfaces to disturb the air. In aerodynamics we are always looking for smoothness. Nirvana for an aerodynamicist is to cut through the air so smoothly that the air is barely ruffled. So all serious pursuit or time-trial riders wear long stretchy socks over their shoes. All the messy surfaces of the rider's shoe and ankle can be tucked neatly away beneath these aero socks. Most of the gains depend on the fabric used, which affects the flow of air around the different parts of the foot, ankle and calf, and how well the seams are hidden.

In trying to find the perfect one to help us achieve our goal, our team bought several types of aero sock that were available on the market and tested them all for their aerodynamic performance. Under our tests none of the products performed as well as their marketing suggested they should. We studied how and why these companies had designed their socks, picked out the good features, discarded the poor features, and in the end designed our own version. We found a specialist company who could help us, briefed them on what we wanted and paid on our trusty credit card. The company assured us we would have the new socks in plenty of time for the National Championships.

Even if a system seems unbeatable, there is always room for improvements, however small. Formula One is a good example: here is a sport in which massive resources are thrown into finding tiny benefits. Formula One cars are the most advanced pieces of automotive technology on the planet. They are designed specifically for the single job of winning Grand Prix. Millions of pounds and years of research and development go into making every part of the car as aerodynamic as possible. When I worked at Mercedes AMG Petronas I spent six months developing the design of the car's wing mirrors. That meant night shifts in the wind tunnel, analysis of the results, then design and development. We'd produce a prototype, take it back to the wind tunnel, analyse it, look for ways to improve it based on the data collected and then produce another prototype. Over and over again. The hours were long. Everyone in the team felt the pressure to deliver results. Even a small gain in aerodynamic efficiency (especially if repeated across the car) could mean the difference between winning and losing.

At that time the Mercedes AMG Petronas team had such a big budget that money was hardly ever considered when looking for improvements in the car. The only constraint was time; if you had an idea that could improve performance the management wanted it for the race cars as quickly as possible. Hence the long hours in the wind tunnel.

In May 2020, after lengthy negotiations with the teams, the sport's governing body, the FIA, announced a cap on annual team budgets of £119m for 2021 onwards. With the biggest teams estimated to be spending more than £300m, this meant significant reductions in personnel and research and development capacity. The budget cap principally aimed to make the sport more financially and environmentally sustainable and meant levelling the playing field between the teams. Formula One is such a highly evolved sport that the principal risk for a big team is intellectual complacency. Teams have become dependent on throwing money at problems and are now being forced to adapt their team culture to be creative on a much smaller budget. The new rules are letting the smaller teams, already used to being innovative on the (relative) cheap, get closer to the podium.

At the other end of the spectrum of sporting technology is the hammer throw. Dating back to the fifteenth century, the hammer throw is one of the original Olympic track and field disciplines. It appeared in the second modern Olympics in 1900 and has been present ever since. After working at Mercedes AMG Petronas, I joined a sports consultancy called Pace Insights where I worked with

British Athletics to help them develop their technology and processes.

The throwing events immediately piqued my interest, particularly the hammer. Here was an event in which a man or woman has to launch a heavy spherical object attached to a wire as far as possible. The athlete is constrained by the size of the circle from which they launch the hammer, but otherwise they can use whatever technique they find most effective. Throughout the modern history of the event, training has focused on finding the optimum swinging technique. That, combined with strength, should give the hammer enough speed to be projected into the air. And that's where the coaching manuals stop. The athlete has let go of the hammer. The flight of the hammer was always assumed beyond their control.

Being fascinated by aerodynamics, my attention was drawn not to the athletes' throwing technique, but to the flight of the hammer. Here was an object subject to the same laws of aerodynamics as a Formula One car or a bike on a velodrome. The athlete had done their bit, propelled it into the air with maximum power. Now the hammer was slowing down. I wanted to understand how it behaved in the air. What impact on its drag did the wire and handle make as they flapped around behind it? How did its aerodynamics affect its trajectory? What role did the wind play in competitions?

In a Formula One team the engineers are expected to understand the FIA rule book, which is a very long and dense read. It is essential to their job because a thorough understanding of the rules allows them to squeeze every last drop of speed, right up to the boundary of what's legal. Another part of my job at Mercedes AMG Petronas was to read the rule book with forensic attention, and write to the FIA seeking clarification on what specific rules meant. Writing such letters was a skill in itself – I could not imply that we were intending to infringe the rules, nor could I give away too much of what we were thinking, as all regulatory enquiry emails had to be published to all teams.

In the hammer throw, the rule book issued by World Athletics is barely a single page of A4. The hammer has to be a sphere. Its size has to be within a specified range. There is a minimum weight but no maximum. The material is specified but there is no detail about surface deformations or finish. There are requirements for the length and diameter of the wire and how the handle is formed. That is about it. When I saw how rudimentary the rules for the hammer design are, my first thought was that they left a great deal of room for optimisation. In other words, I could take my learning from Formula One and apply it to the hammer. Model its flight, analyse what forces were acting upon it, create and test different versions. As far as I could tell, no other country was doing anything like this, so Britain could get an advantage over its Olympic competitors. Sadly, at the time Britain did not have a thrower who was realistically in with a chance of winning an Olympic medal, however aerodynamic their hammer, so the work was shelved.

The point of relating these stories is that whatever the sport, from the extravagant wealth of Formula One to the poor unloved simplicity of the hammer throw, there is always room for improvements. Taken individually they may be small. Aggregated with others, they can be significant. The essential thing to remember is to keep looking. Study how something works, its environment and its set of rules. Think about why something is how it is. And then challenge that thinking. Sometimes you might find that something is the product of years of testing and analysis – a Formula One car's wing mirror. Another time you might find something that, for no reason other than complacency, has never really been challenged – a hammer. The rules state that the hammer has to be spherical. But could it have a dimpled or ribbed surface to improve its aerodynamic performance? What kind of coatings could we apply to the surface to make it faster? If the sphere is filled with a solid substance, what should that be and how heavy? And where should the centre of gravity lie?

These are the kinds of questions that keep me awake at night.

In the last chapter we started to look at how systems have flaws. By studying the system closely you can pinpoint these flaws and come up with alternative approaches. This is certainly helpful. However, if you take the approach of optimising everything, taking nothing for granted, you will naturally begin to exploit those flaws in the system. You don't even need to know what they are.

The position we are taking is that every aspect of our performance can be improved, even if that improvement is tiny. We are constantly seeking to do things better. Always alert to the details.

6

Our Olympics

There is something special about a velodrome. Perhaps it's because most cycle sport takes place on the open road, or out in the wilderness in the case of mountain biking, and can therefore feel somewhat inaccessible to spectators. Velodromes, like football stadiums, are designed for entertainment, for drama. And as a spectator there is that same moment of giddy excitement when, having entered the building and climbed the stairs, you first the see the track below you. The banking looks impossibly steep, the music is pumping, riders are flying round and there is a sense of high energy compressed into the space. In the track centre the riders and their support crews are busy preparing for their races. The area is split into pens and each is filled with bikes, kit bags, rollers and laptops. This is part of what makes track cycling such a fascinating sport to watch. If you wished, you could watch your favourite rider go through their entire preparation routine – the warm-up on the rollers, wriggling into the top half of their skinsuit, pulling on their helmet, applying chalk to their hands for added grip on the handlebars, walking calmly over to the waiting area at trackside and sitting there staring into space, visualising what they need to do, then walking slowly up to the track where their bike is waiting for them...

For the riders, of course, the track centre is a place of work. In training, when the velodrome is empty save for a dozen or so riders and their coaches, it is a place to chat, recover and relax. At a race meet, the presence of spectators and rival riders makes it considerably more tense. From up in the stands it may look like a calm environment but really it is a pressure cooker. Riders handle it in different ways. Some, like Jonny, thrive on the atmosphere, bouncing around to the music and exchanging banter with other teams. I tend to go the other way. Keep my head down, stay focused on the process.

In the two weeks before the 2017 National Championships I experienced a lot of self-doubt. For the previous four months I had been planning and training seriously for three events – the individual pursuit, the kilometre and the team pursuit. In the two individual events I reckoned I had a pretty good chance of a medal, possibly of winning. In the team pursuit, though I was outwardly bullish with the rest of the team, I was less sure. We had only had four weeks of meaningful training together as a squad. Plus, in the team pursuit there was a lot that could go wrong. Execution was a long way from theory.

My training had been going to plan. In every session we did, whether it was on the track or on the road or in the gym, we each had quantifiable targets to achieve. These might be defined in terms of power output, or time spent at a certain heart rate, or repetitions in the gym. Every aspect of my training was measured against a plan, and I had a high level of confidence in my plan. Apart from the odd off day, I had been hitting my targets.

And though the crash in Wales had been a setback for the team, Charlie and I only had superficial injuries and had recovered within a few days. I had no rational reason to doubt myself. Certainly this doubt was a product of the pressure I was putting myself under. I saw this as a big opportunity to make my mark, and it is hard to just take that in your stride without a few wobbles.

As Tipper and I were driving through Derby one afternoon, I mentioned how I was feeling. I said that I felt I wasn't performing as well as I should or could. Tipper did his best to raise my self-confidence by providing an apt analogy.

"It's hard to dig as deep in training as in competition," he said. "Rewind millennia and you're getting chased by a tiger. Then you will dig deep, because your life relies on it. When the competition arrives your body will respond to all of those sensations the way it naturally does, and you'll be able to go deeper than you have before."

It was helpful advice and has stuck with me since. An athlete can train well, and it will probably feel a bit messy and unstructured, but when the moment arrives the body will perform to the level it needs to.

Nevertheless we had prepared our approach well during those four weeks. Everyone knew their role. Our travel and accommodation were meticulously planned. We knew what we were going to eat, when, and who was preparing it. We knew who was pumping tyres and in which gears we were going to ride in each race. Everyone had a printout of a schedule covering every minute of the weekend of the Championships. And in a last-minute boost to morale, our new aero socks arrived on the morning we left for Manchester.

The individual pursuit was on Friday, the kilometre on Saturday. The team pursuit – qualifying and finals, if we got that far, were on Sunday. Jonny was also riding the kilometre. Charlie and Tipper were riding the individual pursuit.

In the weeks leading up to the event I had been working with Mark Keep, a psychologist I first met whilst at university. Mark helped me enormously by showing me the benefit of creating what he called a 'flow state'. The idea of a flow state is not new. It has been around since the 1970s and applied to various fields. Many people call it 'being in the zone'. Elite sports people have retrospectively described themselves as being in a flow state during their biggest successes. However, Mark wanted me to proactively create a flow state. If I could do that all the anxiety would fall away and my performance would be as good as my physiology would allow. In a flow state the athlete is totally immersed in the task at hand, his ego has receded, he is in control, has a positive attitude to the event and knows his abilities align to the needs of the event. Detailed planning underpinned it; if I was in control of every aspect of race day, I could relax into this flow state, knowing I had everything covered.

The qualifying round of the individual pursuit was on Friday morning, then finals in the afternoon. In the minutes leading up to my qualifying ride, all the doubts faded away and were replaced with a kind of laissez-faire attitude. What will be, will be. There was nothing more I could do now, other than perform to the best of my ability. No more training, no more worrying about sleep or diet or equipment. All I had to do now was execute.

The crowd was sparse as I climbed on to my bike. It wasn't like the Olympic finals when the crowd falls silent for an athlete's start; in the early rounds of a competition the crowd keep chatting away, munching on crisps, texting their friends, while the riders in track centre don't pay too much attention either. The announcer uses a rather matter-of-fact tone over the public address system, happy just to impart some basic facts about each rider. None of that mattered to me. I was targeting a time of 4:25 which I thought would be sufficient to get me into the final. My opponent in that qualifying race was Matt Walls, riding for Great Britain; that gave me a little extra incentive to go hard. Walls was not known for riding the individual pursuit but he was a talented multi-discipline rider and a good scalp to take.

I sprinted out of the starting gate and up to full speed, then got into my aerodynamic tuck position. It felt good to finally be here in the race. I poured myself into those opening laps, going slightly too hard. At the early splits I was up on schedule and Walls was falling behind much sooner than I had anticipated. After one kilometre I had him in my sights, and 500 metres later I caught and overtook him. Now the crowd seemed to wake up.

After that I simply tried to hold the same speed, making my legs burn, keeping my breathing deep and regular, ignoring the growing ache in my back and shoulders. Total concentration as I focused on following the black line that marks the shortest way around the track. Into the last laps and I squeezed out every gram of energy I could find into the simple task of pedalling that bicycle as quickly as possible. Bang! The finishing gun fired. I eased up and let my legs spin round. Fastest time... the announcer was calling out. In the back straight I could look up at the scoreboard mounted at one end of the track – 4:22.023. The fastest time so far. I was happy with that. A few minutes later, as I warmed down in the track centre, the remaining few riders finished. No one bettered my time, though Charlie came close. He was second fastest qualifier – we were going to ride against each other in the final.

The wait was long and boring and uneasy. It wasn't worth going back to our rented house so instead I ate a decent lunch, listened to some music, did some stretching and went for a walk around the velodrome. In the track centre and around the velodrome I saw many people that I knew but it was hard to have more than a perfunctory conversation with them. Most of them had been around cycling long enough to know that talking to a rider just before a big race won't elicit much pithy conversation.

When referring to how they feel physically, cyclists will usually refer to their legs. And for all the sports science in the world, there is still some validity to this more intuitive aspect to performance. When I began my warm-up for the final I could feel I had good legs. This helped with my confidence but the nerves were still jangling when I climbed on to my bike on the start line. My first national champion's jersey was there within touching distance, less than five minutes of pain away. On the other side of the track was Charlie. He was my friend and training partner but for now I had to put all that out of my mind.

He pushed me really hard. For lap after lap we were within a second of each other. I told myself not to panic, to maintain my form on the bike. The pain seared through my thighs and calves. My shoulders and neck ached. My mouth was dry. Into the last kilometre and we were still neck and neck. Then Charlie began to fade. One final ragged push for the line and finally I could ease up. As I came around the banking I looked up at the big screen and saw the number one against my name. I had won with a time of 4:22.01. Charlie was four seconds slower. All at once the emotion of what I had achieved came welling up inside me. My first British championship, giving me the right to wear the famous white jersey with blue and red bands. All that training, all those sacrifices, all the self-doubt and anxiety – it had all paid off. Charlie congratulated me, Tipper and Jonny gave the proverbial slap on the back and before I knew it I was being ushered towards the podium.

I had won bike races before, but usually my experience of prize presentations was being given an envelope and a small trophy in a village hall on a Sunday morning. Now there was a sponsored backdrop, bunches of flowers, dignified hands to shake, a sparkly jersey to pull on, the weighty medal around my neck, and an equally sparkly bottle with which to spray Charlie.

I wanted to go out and celebrate but the next day I was due to ride the kilometre time trial. That night I struggled to sleep. My body was full of endorphins and caffeine, and my mind was full of the final, the podium ceremony, the press questions... I couldn't stop gazing lovingly at the national champion's jersey hanging up at the foot of my bed. In the morning, bleary-eyed and stiff in the legs, I went through my usual breakfast routine, though with even more coffee than usual to get me moving. The four of us drove to the velodrome together and prepared to go through it all over again. I knew I had to refocus.

In the kilometre the pain is over much quicker. There are no qualifying rounds, just straight into the final. You get one chance to get it right. From a standing start, you have to use all your strength to get the bike moving, and because you need a big gear this is not dissimilar to doing a deadlift in the gym. Once you have wrestled the bike out of the start, it's a case of getting up to full sprinting speed as quickly as possible, then desperately trying to hold that speed for another 50 seconds or so. Alone on the track, you have no sense of how well you're doing versus the competition. There are no tactical nuances, just a simple and brutal effort.

Elite athletes learn to trust in their process. When I came to the velodrome that second day, even though my mind was swirling from the day before, I knew I could trust in my own preparation process to get me to the start line in the right shape. Every activity that I did between waking up that morning and turning the first pedal stroke was mapped out. It was predictable and boring and routine, and that was just what I needed. My mind could go into that flow state, turning down the volume on all that other psychological noise to just focus on accomplishing the next activity, whether that was eating some rice or tightening up my shoes.

I followed the process and found myself sitting on my bike, staring down the track. Now the confidence buoyed me. I was a national champion in one event, and I could do it in another. You're the fastest, I told myself. Just empty the tanks for one minute, and there will be another gold medal up for the taking. I know it sounds arrogant, but in that position the way you think can influence the outcome. Tell yourself you can do it, and you are more likely to do it.

Whereas the pursuit events are all about creating a harmonious synthesis of man and machine, in the kilometre you always seem to be fighting your bike. I got a good, explosive start but did not go too deeply into my energy reserves in the first 500 metres. Starting too fast and dying horribly in the last two laps is a common mistake. That conservative start allowed me to maintain a high pace into the second half, grimacing and gurning my way through the pain wracking my body. It's cathartic, that kind of pain. And it's over pretty quickly.

I finished with a time of 1:03.02 and after a short wait for the rest of the field to put in their times, I was confirmed as the winner. Another national championship. Another red, white and blue jersey. I felt euphoric. I had never competed at this level before and now I had two championships to my name. My euphoria was turbocharged, so when the cycling media wanted to ask about the team pursuit, and whether the triple was possible for me, I went totally off-script.

"We've done some good times in training. We've got the legs. Come at us, GB," I said, adding, "I think they've got to come and beat us on Sunday."

Shortly after that, the popular website *Cycling Weekly* published an article titled 'Brother NRG team throw down the gauntlet to British Cycling squad at National Track Champs'. When my team-mates saw my exuberant comments they groaned. The plan had been to come into the team pursuit as quietly as possible, to catch British Cycling unawares. That evening in our Airbnb house I took on the chin a fair amount of good-natured abuse. I had proven myself as a racer but in my handling of the media I had a lot to learn.

The next morning everyone was tense. We needed to get the qualifying round out of the way, mainly to instil some confidence in ourselves. Stepping on to the track as one of a team of four is a very different feeling to doing so alone. It is a shared endeavour. The pressure shifts from not letting yourself down to not letting your friends down. We all knew that if we executed our plan we stood a chance of a medal, but we'd never been in this position before, with thousands of spectators watching, photographers clicking away, television commentators reading out our names.

I was more nervous before that team pursuit qualifying round than before either of the two finals I had ridden in earlier in the weekend. I felt responsible for our performance. I had been the driving force behind getting the team together, and many of my ideas had gone into our preparation. The other three had put their lives on hold to pursue this project. I knew we had a good performance in us, but I equally knew that one mistake could bring the whole enterprise to a quick and embarrassing end.

I need not have worried. The qualifying ride went brilliantly to plan. Tipper's analogy about escaping from lions proved to be valid for all four of us, individually and collectively. We all got more out of ourselves, and we rode flexibly as a unit, working together to keep the pace high and consistent. During the race I had a fleeting sense that something was different. There was a new edge to our riding. Perhaps it was the adrenaline of competition. Perhaps it was just that we were going significantly faster than we ever had before. Whatever it was, I was hooked.

We finished with a time of 4:08.4, the quickest we had ever recorded. A few minutes later we were astonished to see that the British Cycling Senior Academy squad, 100% ME (a slightly naff name that promotes the education programme of the UK anti-doping authority) had posted a time of 4:13.2. We had qualified fastest, and 100% ME were second, which meant that we would face them in the final. It also meant we had silver medals guaranteed.

Our qualifying time, and my wayward comments in the press, had the effect of waking British Cycling from their slumber of complacency. Suddenly they realised they had a fight on their hands for the gold medal they assumed was theirs for the taking. Their mechanics dug out their fastest wheels and swapped them on to the 100% ME bikes.

As the race neared, the velodrome filled up with spectators. I was buzzing – with nerves, endorphins and a fair amount of strong coffee. Yet I also felt calm. Mark's work had helped me a great deal. Everything was under control, and I knew exactly what I was supposed to be doing for every minute leading up to the starting pistol being fired. Jonny was less calm. He had decided that his rear wheel was not up to the job of a team pursuit final (not enough lateral strength, he said) and with only 20 minutes to go he was running around the track centre begging people to lend him a better wheel. He got one, fixed it into his bike and made his way to the start line. In the last few minutes the velodrome announcer began to hype the event, calling it a David vs Goliath clash, reading out the names of the eight riders.

The rest of the team looked as nervous as I felt. We couldn't see our opponents clearly because they were on the other side of the track. I'd raced against some of them before, though never at this level, and I could imagine the pressure they were feeling. The British Cycling head coach, Iain Dyer, stood watching his team's final preparations. He had been an instrumental figure in the British Cycling track set-up stretching back to the Athens Olympics in 2004. For him, the National Championships were probably a rather quaint event, unimportant when compared to World Cups, World Championships and Olympics, but – so I imagined – useful for spotting new talent. I wasn't so naïve as to believe I'd be getting a phone call on Monday asking me to join the Olympic programme, but I did consider that my double national titles might at least pique some interest.

The electronic beeps counted us down. With a huge effort, we got our bikes rolling and up to cruising speed. Once we were in full flight all the nerves evaporated. Total focus on the race. Our pacing wasn't perfect, moving between 14.3 and 14.8 seconds per lap, but as the race went on we began to edge a small advantage on the 100% ME team. With his turn done, Jonny dropped off after six of the 16 laps. We pressed on. The finishing time was irrelevant; all that mattered was winning, whatever the margin. I knew that if it was close in the final lap the other team could put in a final dash and snatch it away from us, so Charlie and I piled on the pressure, hoping that Tipper could hang on. Coming off the final banking and into the finishing straight we came alongside each other, sprinting to the line. The gun fired for us, then, a fraction of a second later, it fired for 100% ME. As I punched the air I could hear the roar of the crowd. We'd done it. We had taken on British Cycling and beaten them.

The 100% ME riders were not pleased. When they rolled into their enclosure in the track centre, some of them slumped on to chairs, while some of them started angrily throwing things around. One of them even threw a bike. They were emotionally invested in the race, and perhaps they already knew that this might damage their careers. Their coaches were silent, shocked. As he watched us celebrating, Iain Dyer was heard to say, "Look at those guys celebrating; you'd think they'd won the Olympics."

Of course, for us this was the Olympics. It was the pinnacle of the sport for where we were at that time. We had come from nowhere to being national champions. We celebrated like Olympic champions because we had achieved the grand ambitions we had set for ourselves.

* * *

Our winning time of 4:04.1 was 21 seconds faster than the first full four-kilometre time that we had posted four weeks before, and showed just what we were capable of when carried along by the pressure and adrenaline of high-level competition.

During the medal ceremony we were so fully pumped with adrenaline and endorphins that we behaved much more riotously than was normal for such occasions. We mugged for the cameras, did daft poses and waved to the appreciative crowd. Beside us the 100% ME team just looked like they wanted to go home.

After the melee of the medal ceremony and press interviews (in which my exuberance was this time entirely justified) we sat down with a drink and looked at where that time put us in the context of the Olympics. In Rio 2016, Great Britain won the gold medal in a time of 3:50.3, narrowly beating Australia. Of the eight teams, China finished last, with a time of 4:03.7.

So, in only a few weeks, with a team of journeymen, we had recorded a time that was only fractionally slower than eighth place in the Olympics. We were as stunned as everyone watching in the velodrome that day.

Talk soon turned to the future. We agreed that we had something here with potential. How much faster could we go? At the National Championships we had executed perfectly, but there was still so much more to improve on. In my mind was a long list that, given more time and money, could surely enable us to beat that 4:04 time – the 'optimise everything' list. It would be crazy to walk away now. The next level of competition was the World Cup circuit. We began looking up the results for recent World Cup rounds and concluded that it would take a time of around 3:57 to get on the podium at most rounds. As I drove south from Manchester to head home, exhausted but happy, that time swirled around in my head. To step up again, and by such a margin, felt daunting. But not impossible.

Back at Derby velodrome a few days later, the four of us met up again and sat around in the track centre, discussing what to do next.

That we would keep going was agreed quickly. That we had more potential was clear. The trickier question was how to get ourselves into the next level of competition. From his road racing career, Tipper had some knowledge about the administration of setting up a team at international level. It's not just a case of phoning up the UCI and asking them for a team licence, he said. It's bloody complicated, and expensive. To set up a road team you have to pay a hefty fee and prove that you have enough sponsorship to fund the team.

On checking the UCI website, the good news was that the fee for a track team was only £3,000. The bad news was that we had missed the deadline for the following season by three months. Still, it was worth a try. I emailed the UCI coordinator and asked whether we could still apply. Of course, she replied – just get your application form and funds over to us within two weeks. The door was opening; we knew we would not have too much difficulty getting some sponsorship – we had already been working with some cycling brands and local Derby companies. And even if nothing came of these discussions, ultimately we could put up the money ourselves. We all agreed that £750 each to ride a World Cup was a worthwhile investment, and now we had a new goal. Hopefully the UCI would take a credit card.

* * *

At the National Championships among our support crew was Ellie Green. At the time Ellie was doing her A levels and had ambitions to study sports science at university. Through her father's Nottingham bike shop, Langdale Lightweights, Ellie had long been involved with local club riders, and helping us now offered her exposure to athletes competing at a higher level. Our relationship was mutually supportive – she helped us at races and we helped her studies by providing some real-life sporting scenarios. Sadly, Ellie's mother passed away in 2011 after a long battle with leukaemia. A year later Ellie and her family wanted to create something positive in Karen's memory, so in 2012 the Karen Green Foundation was established. Its aim was to raise money to provide quality holiday accommodation for leukaemia patients and their families, giving them some much-needed relief.

Through Ellie we began to have conversations with Cat Wynne, the manager of the foundation, about the possibility of the Karen Green Foundation sponsoring us. It was one of those serendipitous moments that you later look back on with deep gratitude. In 2017 the foundation was at a turning point in its development and needed to raise its visibility. We needed a relatively small amount of money to set us off on our World Cup journey. Furthermore, by supporting our project, the foundation was able to give Ellie some support in her own career ambitions. We agreed on an initial sponsorship amount of £5,000. For this the foundation got national and international publicity, and for us it meant a UCI licence plus some travel expenses. The next few days were filled with the frantic business of UCI administration and organising the foundation to make a payment of £3,000 into a random Swiss bank account that was apparently linked to the UCI. The following week the UCI got in contact to say that our application had been successful. Team KGF was now officially a UCI-registered international track team.

In six months we would be competing in Poland at our first international race. Now we had a new, and much more challenging, end to start at.

Part 2

Take it apart

7

How reverse engineering can win a war

Berlin, early summer, 1939. An American engineer called Paul Pleiss was about to finish an engineering project and, sensibly, wanted to return to the United States. First, however, he wanted some adventure, so he and a German colleague decided to take an overland trip to India. They got hold of an automobile chassis and built a vehicle they thought would be suited to the distance and the rugged terrain they would face. Just before they left Berlin, they realised that they had no means of carrying water. So the German engineer went to Tempelhof Airport, where he had access to thousands of fuel canisters, and took three. With the canisters filled with water and strapped underneath the car, the two intrepid engineers set off.

They made it across 11 countries without incident and only when they got to India did the Germans catch up with them. Field Marshal Göring sent a plane to bring the German engineer back to

Berlin, but before he left, the engineer gave his American friend a complete set of technical specifications for the manufacture of the fuel containers. He understood just how important in the coming war these canisters, originally named Wehrmacht-Einheitskanister, would become. Their design and manufacture, all under a cloak of secrecy, had been an important part of Hitler's militarisation. The Führer and his generals knew that their plans for a Blitzkrieg advance across Europe required rapid fuel deployment. Tanker trucks were efficient at carrying fuel, but were wholly inadequate in the chaos of a warzone. The Wehrmacht-Einheitskanister (Armed Forces Unit Canister) was a piece of design genius. It carried five gallons of fuel and was constructed of two interlocking pieces of steel, held together with one long weld and lined with plastic to avoid leaks. Ridges and indentations were built into the sides to strengthen the structure and to allow for some expansion and contraction of the fuel. The canister was a neat rectangular shape to enable stacking. And the designers realised that being able to move these canisters around was critical to their usage, so they created three stamped and rounded handles. This meant that the loaded canisters could be passed down a line of soldiers, or that a strong soldier could carry two canisters in each hand. The cap was an integrated lever mechanism (no screw-on cap to lose) and finally, the canisters were produced in different colours to denote different contents – petrol, oil, water etc.

In comparison, the fuel canister being used by the Allies was hopeless. Constructed of four sheets of metal, it was welded together but unlined, making it more flimsy and greatly increasing the likelihood of leaks. There was a single, uncomfortable handle. Removing or replacing the cap required a wrench, pouring from the canister required a spout and filling it required a funnel. British and American soldiers often only used their canisters once before converting them into rudimentary stoves, or filling them with sand to use as makeshift sandbags.

Pleiss continued to Calcutta, put the car into storage and returned to the United States. When the war started he contacted the military and told them about the German fuel canisters. He did not get much of a response, so he organised for the car to be shipped from India to New York. When it arrived in the summer of 1940 the three canisters were still attached and Pleiss immediately sent one to the War Office. The United States military studied the canister and redesigned it, but did so in such a way as to make the end product a great deal weaker. Meanwhile Pleiss travelled to London for his job and talked to British engineers about the German canister. The British were more familiar with its capability, having seen them in action in Norway in April 1940. They were keen to get hold of one, so Pleiss had the second of his three canisters shipped over. The British got to work straight away to dismantle and recreate the canister that became known as the jerrycan.

Frustratingly for those who understood the enormous benefits of the jerrycan, it took two years for the British to put them into mass production. The war in North Africa, in particular, was heavily reliant on fuel; many Allied units were unable to make or maintain territorial gains simply because they ran out of petrol. And ultimately that cost lives. By 1943, however, there were thousands of jerrycans in circulation, and production ramped up in preparation for D-Day. Though the reverse engineering of this simple and effective item took too long to get going, in the end it played a significant role in the Allied victory.

* * *

Reverse engineering has something of a chequered history. Many of its most well-known examples, such as the jerrycan, are connected to war. Since the advent of modern weapons – roughly since the Industrial Revolution – competing forces have wanted to get their hands on each other's secret technology. In 1944 three American B-29 bombers were forced to land in Soviet territory and were taken to Moscow, where Stalin ordered his engineers to make exact copies for the Soviet air force. One of the planes was dismantled, one used for flight testing and one kept mothballed for reference. Under pressure from Stalin, over 900 factories were involved in the effort to reverse engineer the American planes, then build a Soviet copy. The design work, which involved making 105,000 drawings, was completed in less than a year, and a year later the first 20 Soviet versions, called the Tu-4, rolled off the production line. The first test flight was a success and over the coming years a whole generation of Tu bombers played an integral part in the Soviet Union's Cold War defences.

In this sort of military scenario, the model for reverse engineering is straightforward – somehow get hold of your enemy's technology, dismantle it, copy it and finally use that copy against your enemy. Ethics don't come into the equation. In the history of

Formula One there has been a similar mentality. Every team would love to get hold of their opponent's superior car, take it apart and build a copy. Because that is not feasible (not to mention illegal), they have to make do with spy photographs of cars being tested and poaching the other team's staff.

Military technology, like Formula One cars, has become exponentially more complex in the last 30 years as we have moved from the industrial to the information age. A 2019 MIT study by Andrea and Mauro Gilli argued that this increase in technological complexity has made it increasingly hard to reverse engineer, or imitate, the best-in-class weapons, which are generally produced by the United States. For example, in a modern fighter jet, everything is controlled by software. The F-4 Phantom II (1958) had some rudimentary software, with 1,000 lines of code. The latest incarnation of the same plane, the F-35 Joint Strike Fighter has 5.6 million lines of code. Such planes are systems of systems, and utilise some of the most advanced software in the world. This software is connected to advanced and precise engineering that is highly sensitive and therefore prone to malfunction if even the smallest part is wrong. Even if a Chinese design team got hold of an F-35, the physical plane would only tell them part of the story. Replicating its operating software would require an immense cyber-espionage effort.

In the first half of the twentieth century, it was relatively easy to imitate an opponent's technology. An experienced team of engineers could dismantle something, such as the B-29 bomber, and use generic engineering knowledge to work out how to imitate it. The principal obstacle was not designing a prototype but putting that prototype into large-scale production. For example, the rivalry of naval fleets, such as between Britain and Germany, was based on building faster, stronger ships. In the 1920s, Imperial Japan was able to join this arms race by investing time, energy and money into copying the British Dreadnought warships. Japan could do so because they had the resource to throw at the problem.

By the end of the twentieth century, however, generic engineering knowledge was not enough. Weapons technology is complex and so specialised that nations intent on imitation would need the same level of scientific infrastructure (laboratories, testing and production facilities) just to start the job. Crucially, they would also need the same level of specialist knowledge among their design team.

How does this relate to pedalling a bicycle around a wooden track? Well, it is important to note that the kind of reverse engineering I applied to track cycling is not about imitation. I do not want to get hold of a national team's bikes, or their wind tunnel test results, or their training session spreadsheets, then copy them in the hope of putting together the same result. I don't want to do this because I would be assuming they are the optimal way of doing things. A dangerous mistake. Never assume that the competition has got it all figured out. Scratch the surface and you will soon discover otherwise. My approach is to reverse engineer the event, not our rivals. In other words, set the goal around achieving a certain level of performance, then work out how to get there.

This is also a much more comfortable ethical position. Reverse engineering (many of its modern applications are in the world of software) is not illegal but historically it has verged on the murky world of corporate espionage. I am not concerned with stealing secrets from our competition. My focus is on how to disassemble a goal and then plot a course towards success. In a competitive environment, such as sport, there is no need to worry about the competition. For the moment at least, they are irrelevant.

8

Be open to ideas sex

In cycling, as in other sports, the knowledge that underpins high performance is passed around in a haphazard fashion. Coaches, soigneurs, mechanics and nutritionists move between teams, taking their nuggets of go-faster information with them. And the more progressive teams bring in new support staff from outside the sport, hoping for a fresh pair of eyes. The vast majority of these support staff are professional, highly qualified people.

Cycling has become a lot more adept at using science – for example, how to use nutrition to fuel specific training and racing strategies – but cycling still isn't very good at thinking scientifically about *holistic* performance. A team might use science to enhance several specific aspects of their riders' performance, and they might even use science (sometimes unwittingly) to enhance hundreds of aspects of their riders' performance. But they don't approach the whole event with a scientific frame of mind. That's because to apply the rigour of science to the whole event requires taking a mental step backwards. It requires the proverbial blank sheet of paper. You have to – as we are about to explore in the following chapters – start from first principles. Break down the event into its component parts and then put it back together again, probably in a new way.

National and professional teams are staffed by people with years of experience in the sport. Often they will boast about the hundreds of years of combined experience they have in the team. All that experience translates to knowledge, and that knowledge is essential for the day-to-day business of running a professional sports team. Without it, disaster on a basic operational level would not be far away. Imagine replacing all of a school's teachers with parents. How long before the school descended into chaos?

Knowledge gained through experience is fundamental to getting a complicated job done. But because the knowledge is based on the past, on older ways of working, it can become a limitation. A team of experienced professionals will always look for incremental improvements, not believing that dramatic improvements are possible. There is a kind of arrogance at work here – the mentality that if you are experienced, you are therefore at the top of your game with little more to learn. The fresh thinking we are striving for only becomes possible if either the experienced professionals are truly open to redesigning their approach from first principles, or (much more likely) someone new comes along with new ideas – and delivers.

You could call it ideas sex. Biologically speaking, sex is about two different genetic identities coming together to create a new genetic identity. Ideas work the same way. Fertilisation between different sources will create new ideas. Fertilisation between two sources with the same genetic identity will create nothing new, and may hinder evolution. We might call this ideas incest. Never a good thing.

A good example of ideas sex is one of the measures introduced by Tim Kerrison at Team Sky. Kerrison, an Australian, started his career as a rower. Realising that he would not make it to the pinnacle of the sport, he switched to coaching, first the Australian rowing team, then the elite swimming team. He later moved to the British Swimming team and then in 2009 to Team Sky. In cycling, Kerrison saw what he has called a 'culture gap' – that is, a sport with a gap between how it was doing things and the best sports science of the day. For anyone who could step in and bridge that gap, that was an opportunity. Crucially Kerrison joined Team Sky early enough in their evolution that he was able to shape the team's thinking. Brailsford and his staff were keen to introduce new ideas to road racing. The innovative approach of Chris Boardman's Secret Squirrel Club was the prevailing attitude. If they could do it on the Olympic velodromes, why not the roads of the Tour de France?

During his first year, which was also Team Sky's first year as a racing team, Kerrison mainly kept a watching brief. He was new to the sport and wanted to learn before suggesting ways to change it. One of the quirks he noticed was that riders never warmed down after a race. They would warm up on a stationary trainer (though only if a fast start was expected), but never warm down. Which meant that they were finishing a race with an intense effort, then going straight to the team bus, media interviews or the podium.

Their bodies were going from maximum effort to zero effort in the space of a few minutes. Physiologically this was not ideal. Athletes' bodies need to warm down in a carefully calibrated arc. Doing so helps recovery, an essential part of being a Tour de France cyclist because you have to get up tomorrow and do it all over again. Warming down also allows the riders to decompress psychologically. Rather than go straight into a media scrum, they get a few precious minutes to bring the adrenaline levels down, to reflect on what has happened in the race and to speak to their coach.

Before Kerrison came along, professional cyclists understood the benefits of warming down. It was standard practice in any intense training session. After the last sprint or hill climb a rider would ride home at an easy level, spinning their legs on an easy gear. Instinctively the riders knew this was the right thing to do for their legs, though many mistakenly thought that they were getting rid of lactic acid from their muscles. In fact, they were clearing metabolites and bringing those muscles back to a balanced state. So the knowledge was out there, even if it wasn't always grounded in science. It was just that no one had thought to apply this method to the race scenario. Everyone did things the old way – sprint to the finish, get off your bike.

Perhaps it was just that Kerrison and Brailsford were brave enough to stand up to race organisers and members of the press, to tell them that the riders needed 10 minutes on their stationary trainers before any interviews or jersey presentations could take place. Many other teams ridiculed Kerrison's innovation. Now they all do it.

Cross-discipline collaboration is increasingly common in science. In recent years there has been a recognition that the global challenge of environmental catastrophe requires scientists to work together across subjects that traditionally remained in their silos. Diversity of perspectives can bring new insights to a problem. It can also create a multi-faceted solution. In academia, working in such a way is not without its challenges; early career scientists are encouraged to stay strictly within their disciplines before branching out because their superiors want them to develop their careers in a linear fashion. Working across disciplines can feel uncomfortable – there are new environments, language and skills to learn, so it takes some courage to plunge oneself into it. Yet ultimately it will almost certainly be a rewarding experience.

In business, the same thinking has been used by innovators such as Apple's Steve Jobs. When Jobs' team began working on the iPod, a product that would revolutionise the consumer technology industry, he was careful to organise Apple as one flexible business unit. This was in direct contrast to Apple's main competitor Sony, who were organised into several semi-autonomous divisions. Jobs wanted a multi-disciplinary team with a shared objective and one set of metrics. Sony had multiple teams, split by discipline, all working towards slightly different objectives. Apple had an environment that encouraged creativity whereas Sony's structure only encouraged bureaucracy.

Sub-optimal performance comes from accepting things the way they have always been done. Have the confidence to be open to ideas sex. Look for fresh perspectives on your project. In the next chapter I am going to look at taking an objective back to first principles, and someone who thinks we could all soon be living on Mars.

9

How to use first principles

On a sunny afternoon on 30 May 2020, crowds gathered on the beaches close to Cape Canaveral, Florida, gazing expectantly at the sky. At 15:22 local time, a slender white rocket blasted off from Kennedy Space Center and headed north-east, out over the Atlantic. After two and a half minutes the lower stage of the rocket, its job done, detached itself and returned to earth, landing on a drone ship. Doug Hurley and Bob Behnken, two veterans of the space shuttle programme, continued into orbit in their Crew Dragon spacecraft, heading for the International Space Station, where they would stay for up to four months.

This was the first manned space flight on a US rocket from US soil since 2011, when NASA's space shuttles were retired. It was an emotional moment; the country had rediscovered its space capability. And it had done so by undertaking a new public-private partnership. NASA does not own the Crew Dragon or the Falcon 9 rocket on which it launched. It simply rents them from a company called SpaceX. It is basically a taxi service into space.

SpaceX has been the butt of many jokes since its inception in 2002. For its founder, Elon Musk, this launch was a vindication of his vision and reward for the effort he has poured into making commercial space travel a reality. Musk is charismatic and driven. He thinks big. SpaceX was formed because Musk believes that impending environmental catastrophe on Earth means the human race needs a back-up plan. His plan is to establish a colony on Mars. In interviews he has said that he wants to die on Mars, and not from a crash landing. Originally from South Africa, Musk graduated from university in California with degrees in physics and economics and straight away began building a business empire. His fortune – now estimated at $46 billion – was kick-started by his creation and subsequent sale of a software business. He then founded, and sold, an online bank, using the proceeds to start SpaceX. His other primary business is Tesla, the innovative electric car manufacturer. Musk's interests are expansive, though all linked. He is involved in developing artificial intelligence systems, brain-computer interface systems, and has created a company to research the boundaries of high-speed travel through tunnels deep beneath the earth.

One of the reasons for Musk's success is that he is not just a CEO who manages his companies and lets others produce the products. He is heavily involved in the design and engineering of all his projects. This is the bit he loves. Though not formally qualified in engineering, he sees himself as an engineer.

Musk is sometimes portrayed in the media as some kind of eccentric genius akin to Tony Stark, Marvel Comics' fictional creator of Iron Man. There is a video on YouTube that purports to walk the viewer through Musk's average day, and if you watch it the principal thing you learn is that he works very, very hard. There are no weird activities. He simply works a long day and squeezes in time to spend with his children, going to the gym, reading. Much like the rest of us, in fact.

What does set Musk apart is his belief in a specific way of thinking.

During the two years he spent as an undergraduate at Queen's University in Ontario, Canada, Musk learnt what is known as the Socratic method. He has said, "One particular thing that I learned at Queen's – both from faculty and students – was how to work collaboratively with smart people and make use of the Socratic method to achieve commonality of purpose."

Named after the Greek philosopher Socrates, who lived from 470 to 399 BC, the Socratic method centres on asking open-ended questions in pursuit of deeper understanding. This could be as specific as enquiring into how a space rocket works, or as wide-ranging as how humans should live their lives. The Socratic method calls for a continual thirst for knowledge and self-improvement. Nothing should be taken for granted. Everything can and should be questioned. It is a more grown-up equivalent of the child who continually asks why. In children this is usually just a phase. Whatever you say, they ask why. But why? It is cute at first, then annoying. And yet it is very similar to the Socratic method. It's just that as adults we have learnt to accept the answers that are given to us. We stop asking why.

At SpaceX Musk had a clear objective – space travel to Mars. At first he began asking the existing space powers, Russia and China, how much it would cost to buy one of their rockets. He was quoted astronomical figures which, even if he'd been able to afford them, were not sustainable in the long term. Musk thought through his objective and realised that the key to achieving sustainable space travel lay in significantly reducing the costs of the hardware. Not only did he have a limited budget, he also understood that creating a commercially viable space travel system was critically important. No one had ever considered market economics in relation to space travel before. It had always been a venture funded by governments from defence budgets. In the USA that is a very deep pocket.

Using the Socratic method, Musk began questioning everything we know about space rockets. He dismantled – theoretically – the existing technology of the Chinese and the Soviets, breaking it down into its component parts, then further down into its base materials. He realised through research that a rocket is primarily made of carbon fibre, space-grade aluminium, copper and other metals. Then he worked out how much that combination of materials would cost if bought direct from a London Metals Exchange. It was a fraction of the price, so he invested heavily in those, but of course he only had a big pile of metal, not a machine to fly. The next step was to work with his team to find innovative ways to build a rocket at a significantly reduced cost.

They took the whole process of launching rockets back to first principles. Putting aside all previous thinking, they reduced the problem to its fundamentals. What were the laws of physics governing space travel? How did atmospheric conditions affect the rocket's performance? What was required to get a rocket safely off the launch pad, then into orbit? How much time would that take to develop and how much would it cost?

One of the programme's most eye-catching solutions was creating reusable rockets. Before SpaceX, the booster rockets that propelled astronauts into orbit would be destroyed in the process of detaching and falling back to earth. SpaceX developed a first-stage booster rocket whose descent could be controlled to the point where it could be landed on a specific landing pad, or a drone ship out at sea. SpaceX's booster rockets can now be used up to 10 times before becoming defunct, and the engineers are working on making many other components of the process reusable.

With all of these innovations, not only has SpaceX succeeded in revitalising the American space programme, its coalescence of science and business has brought in significant revenue. It has been ferrying cargo to the International Space Station on behalf of NASA for over a decade, using its Dragon capsules atop Falcon 9 booster rockets. Supply contracts with NASA have reportedly brought in over $1.6bn. In April 2019 SpaceX signed another deal with NASA, worth $69m, to smash one of its rockets into an asteroid in 2022. Whilst this sounds part wacky scientist idea, part childhood fantasy, it is actually a central part of the Double Asteroid Redirection Test (DART), an initiative by NASA to work out how to redirect potentially dangerous asteroids heading towards Earth. For SpaceX, however, the income from NASA is relatively small compared to its commercial operation. Its contracts to take satellites and military equipment into space have reportedly earned it over $12bn.

Reasoning from first principles means reducing a problem all the way down to its core parts, to the laws that cannot be altered. In space travel these are the laws of physics. In business these are the laws of economics. The problem in hand cannot be reduced any further and the relevant laws are the building blocks on which the Socratic thinker can base his or her ideas. Musk created his own methodology and form of thinking from scratch, taking only the unarguable laws that affect his goal and reinventing everything else.

The opposite to Socratic thinking is thinking by analogy, and Musk would probably say that is how most people operate most of the time. Thinking by analogy simply means iterating what has already been done, where our thoughts are based on a method that already exists. Even if you adopt a method that has been universally rejected, you are still thinking by analogy. You could argue it is lazy, that Socratic thinking is more rigorous and therefore more demanding. But equally you could argue that thinking by analogy is how we are educated, how much of the world works, and therefore it is a default setting for us.

There are other, less daunting, examples of using the Socratic method. When Jonah Peretti founded BuzzFeed in 2006, he wanted his website to be one of the most popular on the internet. Peretti studied the psychology of how stories go viral on social media and realised that the first principle of a website, if what you wanted was a big audience, was wide distribution. High-quality reporting on stories that people should be reading (according to the relevant editor's opinion anyway) was not as important as giving people stories they actually wanted to read. Give them what they want, Peretti decided, and they would share stories on social media, thereby growing the website's profile and traffic. The stories themselves were also reduced to first principles: keep it short, ensure there is a human element, and use a strong and persuasive headline. Hence all those articles we see called something like '21 Times an Actor Almost Saved a Bad Movie by Sheer Force of Will.' You know it is not highbrow but you cannot stop yourself clicking on it.

Whatever you think of Musk and Peretti, the interesting commonality between them is that they both focused on what will work in the market they are working in. They were in the business of making money (though undoubtedly both would claim to have higher goals) and to make money they knew they had to give the customer what they wanted. NASA wanted an American-owned rocket system they didn't have to design and build themselves. Mobile phone users (that is, practically everyone), wanted engaging but undemanding news stories to read in less than three minutes. Musk and Peretti understood the context of their objective and worked with it. Working to first principles is not just a theoretical exercise; it is pragmatic and action-oriented.

* * *

When we won the National Championships, Jacob, Jonny, Charlie and I came a long way from our starting point. But I knew there was still so much more to analyse, so much more to improve. We had begun to break the team pursuit down to its first principles but lack of time had meant we hadn't really questioned every aspect of the event thoroughly. Socrates would not have approved.

In the spring of 2017, with the next World Cup six months away, we had more time to plan. And when we started taking the team pursuit back to first principles, we could see that really there is a single objective: get the third rider to the finish line as quickly as possible.

There are two principles affecting this objective that cannot be changed. The first is the rule book. You have to work within the rules. For example, the UCI track racing regulations clearly state: 'The time and the classification of each team shall be taken on that of the third rider of each team. The time shall be measured on the front wheel of the third rider of each team.'

However, there is a significant caveat: you only have to work within the rules *as they are written down*. The rule book is always open to interpretation. Even in Formula One there is room for interpretation, if you read the book closely enough. And, for the sake of argument, I always stand by the fact that there is no such thing as the 'spirit' of the rules. This notion is sometimes invoked by the relevant authorities to cover up for some shoddy rule drafting, or by a competitor worried that a rival has discovered an opportunity. Using the 'spirit' of the rules as an argument is supposed to appeal to one's moral judgement, yet it is vague and, at worst, dishonest. What matters is what is written down.

The second principle we needed to adhere to is the laws of physics. These are not open to interpretation and they govern every physical action that takes place on the track, so you need to comprehensively understand them.

Beyond these two sets of rules, anything was possible. I have often said that if dressing up in a giant penis costume made me go faster, I would do it. Who cares about what people think of you? The only objective here is to go faster. When I started road racing at national level, I wore aero socks. This was not the done thing in road racing, even though everyone understood that being more aerodynamic makes a cyclist go faster. Tradition was holding the sport back. On the start line of a race in Lancashire on one chilly spring morning, the riders around me began to make jokes about my aero socks. I just shrugged and laughed along with them. A few weeks later these other riders and most of their team-mates began wearing aero socks too.

The fundamental question for the team pursuit became: how do we best use four riders over four kilometres to get the third-placed rider to the finish line as quickly as possible? Looking at the event from the point of view of physics, it all comes down to energy. A rider has energy stored in his body. He transmits that energy into the pedals to propel the bike forward. That is what we call 'power in'. My goal was always to minimise the amount that is lost during the process of transferring the power into movement. The principal ways in which power is lost are riding through the air, rolling resistance (the tyres on the track) and drive-train friction (the friction of the chain on the chainring and sprocket). This is 'power out'. Everything we did as a team had to be in the cause of turning as much of the energy we create as possible into forward speed.

From here, we could easily break the problem down into its component parts:

1. People: physiology and psychology
2. Bikes: strength, weight and aerodynamics
3. Clothing: aerodynamics and comfort
4. Strategy: pace and frequency of changes

These components of the event can all be controlled by us. The aspects that cannot be controlled include the track surface and atmospheric conditions inside the velodrome, but because these aspects affect all teams equally, you could argue that their impact on the result is negligible.

Now that we had our component parts, we could start to brainstorm questions in each section. For example, for the strategy section, we asked:

- How do we get maximum power out from all four riders without dropping the third man?
- How often should we change the lead man?
- Should the rider relinquishing the lead always go to the back?
- How hard are the different riders working when sitting in the line?
- What information do we need during the race in order to adapt our strategy?
- How do we adapt our strategy if one of our riders is in spectacularly good form, or spectacularly bad form?

Forget what has gone before. Establish the first principles that apply to what you are trying to achieve, then channel Socrates to really interrogate every aspect of your challenge. At this stage we do not need answers (though some will inevitably begin popping into your mind), we only need questions. Each question will likely generate a bunch of new questions.

Both Charlie and I had engineering backgrounds and had been taught to think from first principles. Our attitude was always, anything goes. There are no stupid questions. Collaboration will add different perspectives on the challenge. Tipper asked different questions to those I asked because he came at it with a different outlook, a different set of experiences and knowledge.

Asked to think of questions that will break down a problem, we tend to jump straight to solutions. Our questions might have a question mark after them, but we already have a solution in the back of our mind. This is normal. Our brains are eager to find answers. And sometimes the answer is so simple that it immediately shouts at us, "I'm here! I'm here!" It can be difficult to ignore that.

We cannot blot out those answers that lurk behind our questions. So we must hold them loosely. Write them down. Do not grow attached to them, and do not give them the authority they want. At this stage, it's too early in the process to decide what will work and what will not. By going with the answers at this stage you would be making too many assumptions, with scant evidence and no testing. Before we get into finding solutions, though, we must first assess what resource is at our disposal.

Part 3

Assess what you have

10

Top Trumps

To understand our resources, we started with the four categories outlined in the previous chapter: people, bikes, clothing and strategy. Our overarching principle was to break down each category into clearly defined, and ideally measurable, elements. However, each category required a different intellectual approach. Some were practical and material, for example: which wheels do we own? Some were more knowledge-based, for example: how much do we know about training? We worked through the four categories in reverse order.

Strategy. This is something entirely knowledge-based. When assessing our resources, we were really trying to assess our own intellectual capability. Not easy to do objectively. Our experience was limited – only one serious competitive outing and a few weeks of training. In other words, we didn't know what we didn't know. To date we had had one good idea (to change less frequently than the accepted norm) but if we were to become a more flexible and powerful team, we would need more weapons in our armoury. We may not have admitted it at the time but we needed more help in this area.

Clothing. The inventory of what a pursuit rider wears is pretty simple: skinsuit, shoes, socks and oversocks, helmet. The assessment we undertook on our clothing was all about how aerodynamic it was. Many aerodynamicists have attempted to calculate the percentage split of total drag between a rider and his bike. Results are variable and affected by a number of factors, but a good rule of thumb is 80 per cent of the drag is on the rider (i.e. position and clothing) and only 20 per cent on the bike. This shows that spending time and money on a new bike is probably going to be less beneficial than improving riding position – which is also much cheaper. In early 2017 we only had access to the same off-the-peg clothing that anyone could buy, so our tests focused on comparing the performance of those products currently on the market. Finding the best in class was beneficial but every rider has different requirements, a different shape and a different style of riding. Creating something more bespoke to our requirements – as we had done with our aero socks – was our long-term goal. Here was an example of assessing what resource was at our disposal and coming to the conclusion that we needed outside expertise to get to the level of performance we wanted.

Bikes. Cyclists can have very complicated relationships with their bikes. They spend countless hours on their bikes, thinking about their bikes, talking about their bikes. Often it is quite an emotional relationship. We talk about our first bike with nostalgic love. Our bikes are a way for us to channel our feelings, particularly anger. At its best, cycling can be a true synthesis of man and machine. Road cyclists often talk about how a bike 'feels' or 'handles'. I can understand this. A road bike has to cope with a variety of physical challenges and it is underneath a rider for several hours, so comfort and confidence in its handling are important. A pursuit bike is a very different beast. Its sole job is to go fast for four minutes, indoors, on a smooth track. Every component of the bike has to be engineered to make it as aerodynamic as possible, and to efficiently transmit energy from the rider into forward motion. It does not have to be adaptable because it only has a single purpose. Much like a Formula One car. Riding a pursuit bike down to the shops would be as terrifying (and impractical) as trying to drive there in a Mercedes Formula One car.

Like our clothing, at that time we only had access to whichever bikes were on the retail market. It is easy to fall into the trap of equating money with performance, but we had to keep an open mind. The most expensive pair of wheels will not necessarily be the best for the job, for a variety of reasons. An example of this is our helmets. When testing a range of aerodynamic helmets we were rather perplexed to find that the Tempor helmet by Swedish ski and cycle brand POC performed best. The Tempor had been used by professional riders a few years before but was soon dropped from POC's retail range. The reason for this seemed to be the helmet's aesthetic. Aero helmets usually have a teardrop shape, following the curve of the head back to a pointed tail at the nape of the neck. The Tempor did the same but flared out at the sides, making its wearer look like a Star Wars Stormtrooper. Professional riders obliged to wear them during time trials reportedly felt silly, and in cycling retail customers always take their cues from the pros. Despite being the fastest helmet on the market, riders stopped wearing them. It may not have been quite as silly as a giant penis outfit, but the same principle applied.

Through testing we began to understand the capabilities of our bikes. Perhaps more importantly the process led us to understand where further gains might be made, if we could find a way to design and engineer our own components. We did not have – and would never have – the kind of budget that allows national teams to design and build entirely new bikes from scratch, but then we did not believe that was necessary. A more practical arrangement was to work in partnership with industry experts. We found those who could work hand in hand with us on development, provide data to guide the project, create the final product and help us to utilise it. We became adept at doing this quickly so that the development cycle was a matter of weeks, instead of months or years. We got very fast at getting better.

People. The most challenging, and rewarding, kind of resource to attempt to understand. What we were after was a holistic view of each member of the team. Not only their physiology but also their psychology, how they interact within the team, and even practical aspects such as where they live. It is essential to be realistic. This is an exercise in understanding whom you have in the team, not whom you wish you have. Anyone who has joined a new company as a manager will recognise the process of getting to know the existing team, and trying not to waste time dreaming of some other perfect group of people.

Again, the approach is to break down the analysis into a set of specific measures. Though the fundamental rules of physiology are the same, each sport will have its own measures, depending on the demands placed on the athlete. Over the last 10 years, power has become the central way that cyclists measure performance. We look at power output during the event or training session, and we also look at how much power we save through aerodynamic changes. Power is expressed in watts, so you may hear a rider talking about their new wheels saving them 10 watts. A rider in a team pursuit at international level will be putting out an average of 450 watts over the four minutes.

Once you understand the relative power of the four riders, you can start to see different strategies that may work. We used a model called Critical Power to help us define the most efficient strategy for our team, and it can work for any given group of riders too. Critical Power is an expression of the amount of energy you can produce over a given time, typically 30 to 60 minutes. A trained cyclist could ride at this level with some degree of comfort but would know that to increase the power output would quickly result in a maximal effort that could not be maintained for long. Part of the Critical Power model is a variable called W Prime, which I think of as a tank of anaerobic energy. This tank is finite. During a race or training session the rider is either draining or refilling that tank depending on their level of exertion. A rider working at or below their Critical Power level can raise their energy output, but their capacity to do so is also finite. With the right data, this capacity to work above Critical Power can be calculated for every individual in the team.

For example Jonny had large W Prime but a very low Critical Power – the maximum sustainable power for a given time. That means the longer he stays in the race, the more he is draining his finite tank of anaerobic energy. This allows him to produce very high powers for short durations, but in longer efforts, before everyone else, he will completely deplete his W Prime and be unable to continue to produce the required power output, soon slowing himself and the team. This will happen even if he has the aerodynamic advantage of sitting at the back of the line because he is working above his critical power. A rider sitting in the line is not contributing anything to making the team go faster, and if they are using up their finite tank of anaerobic energy as they do so, when they find themselves on the front they will have much less energy than they need to help the team maintain their speed. So, to turn this quality into a positive, we can look at a different way for Jonny to contribute to the team. Over five laps, he is capable of putting in a huge effort at high power levels. So why not use him for the first five of 16 laps, then he can swing off and leave the other three to finish the job? This plan also means that the other three of us have a consistent pace to follow over those first six laps, with no surprising surges. Knowing that provided a lot of psychological comfort to the others on the team.

Indeed, over the years this role has become Jonny's trademark. I lead the team away from the start, do one and a quarter laps on the front to get us up to full speed, then swing off to let Jonny take over. His job is surprisingly complex. He does five laps on the front, trying to get the other three of us deep into the race as fresh as possible. This means he has to very carefully judge his effort. Go too slowly and he could throw the race away. Go too fast and he would put the rest of us in trouble. There would be no point in him dragging us around for five lightning laps, only for us to die over the remaining nine. All of which means that when Jonny is on good form, when he gets on the front, he has to remind himself not to go too hard. His effort is sub-maximal, which means he could go a lot harder, but that would probably destroy the team's performance. As his five laps comes towards an end, Jonny uses his judgement to decide when to swing off. The worst scenario was that he would begin to fade, the pace would slow (we call it parking) and then, when he did swing, the rest of the team would need to re-accelerate. That would be a painful experience and seriously damage our chance of winning the bike race.

Do you remember the game Top Trumps? Two players divide a pack of cards equally, then on each turn compare a vital statistic, the aim of the game being to trump your opponent's card. If track racing had a deck of Top Trump cards, British Cycling would have 10 packs. Their principal problem would be how to hold all the cards in their hand. British Cycling are able to pick riders from a far bigger gene pool so they can afford to be choosy. Other nations have always followed British Cycling's methods, so theoretically the country with the biggest gene pool will win. If the United States followed British Cycling's methodology, with its access to thousands of Top Trump packs, it would win everything.

My team, on the other hand, had just four cards:

Name: Dan Bigham

Date of birth: 02/10/1991

Height (cm): 183

Weight (kg): 76

Peak power: 1550

Track technical ability: 90

Fatigue tolerance: 55

Training morale: 70

Race morale: 95

General morale: 80

Innovation: 90

Positivity: 105

Aerobic power: 70

Anaerobic power: 85

Washing-up ability: 10 (my biggest weakness, I hate it)

Aerodynamics: 90

Cookery skills: 35

Name: Charlie Tanfield

Date of birth: 17/11/1996

Height (cm): 190

Weight (kg): 80

Peak power: 1350

Track technical ability: 80

Fatigue tolerance: 95 (the Tanfields have trained themselves to
never suffer from fatigue – ever)

Training morale: 70

Race morale: 90

General morale: 80

Innovation: 90

Positivity: 75

Aerobic power: 90

Anaerobic power: 50

Washing-up ability: 50

Aerodynamics: 85

Cookery skills: 35

Name: Jacob Tipper

Date of birth: 02/12/1991

Height (cm): 183

Weight (kg): 78

Peak power: 1550

Track technical ability: 75

Fatigue tolerance: 75

Training morale: 20 (Tipper lived off a supply of chocolate
biscuits to keep his morale up)

Race morale: 30

General morale: 5

Innovation: 90

Positivity: 2 (the king of finding the one tiny flaw in your argument)

Aerobic power: 70

Anaerobic power: 85

Washing-up ability: 95

Aerodynamics: 60

Cookery skills: 50

Name: Jonny Wale

Date of birth: 15/06/1991

Height (cm): 183

Weight (kg): 85

Peak power: 1800

Track technical ability: 40

Fatigue tolerance: 70

Training morale: 10 or 100 (depending on the day – we just prayed we got the good days)

Race morale: 10 or 100 (depending on the day – we just prayed we got the good days)

General morale: 10 or 100 (depending on the day – we just prayed we got the good days)

Innovation: 90

Positivity: 75

Aerobic power: 50

Anaerobic power: 95

Washing-up ability: 70

Aerodynamics: 75

Cookery skills: 95 (brilliant cook but 5 points deducted for not cooking enough)

Of course, we are all more complicated than a Top Trumps card. Psychology is incredibly important for an elite athlete, and while it can be analysed, it cannot be objectively measured. What you should always be looking for is honesty – for individuals to be honest with themselves and with the team. In the following chapter we will look at how a group of individuals can become a team.

A cycling team is not just the riders, it also extends to those around you, professional support staff and family and friends. It might seem a little cold to take an audit of your family and friends but it is essential at this stage to understand what resource is available to support your project. Perhaps your family are not really as supportive as they could be, or they lack the energy, the skills or the drive to give meaningful support. That's okay. Don't be disheartened. Just make a note of it (mentally, if you want to keep your plans secret!) and move on. There are ways around every problem.

Remember that not every deficit is a disadvantage. We couldn't afford to pay a mechanic so we did our own wrenching (as it's called in cycling). The benefit was that we got to know the details of our bikes, and we took responsibility for our bike being in perfect condition so we didn't worry about whether the mechanics had made a mistake. Sometimes, in the heat of competition or training, having a simple mechanical task to complete is a useful way to take your mind off the racing.

The final resource to look at is the one that people do not like to talk about – money. Running a professional cycling team was not cheap. British Cycling has UK Sport funding running into the millions, the majority of which is focused on track-racing success at the Olympics. Between the four of us in Team KGF we had the Karen Green Foundation sponsorship money, a few thousand in savings, stratospheric student loans to pay back (eventually), and some shiny new credit cards. Before the Karen Green Foundation stepped in with their sponsorship, we had discussed paying for the UCI fee ourselves, which would have been £750 each. This seemed to us a good price if it paid for the opportunity to ride World Cups, but it wouldn't be the end of what we would have to pay for.

When we sat down to discuss, we decided to split the budget into three categories. Firstly, expenses. These are the costs incurred simply by taking part – entry fees, travel, accommodation and velodrome fees for training sessions. Secondly, technology. Bikes are the biggest chunk of this, but we also have laptops, cameras, measurement sensors and software. Thirdly, and potentially the biggest chunk of the three, is the cost of people. If you are fortunate enough to be selected to join the British Cycling Olympic Development Programme, you will be paid a salary. The programme also has to pay a good wage to every coach, mechanic, bike designer, engineer, bio-mechanic, data analyst, skinsuit manufacturer, nutritionist, masseur and psychologist... the list is very long. So, while the British Cycling budget sounds impressive, the majority (quite rightly, because these are professional people) goes on its staff. In Team KGF we fulfilled all the roles above, for free. We poured all our time into the project because we loved it, not for financial gain. Yes, we needed enough money to eat, pay the rent and pay the bills. But it wasn't so long before that we'd been students. We just carried on that frugal lifestyle, albeit with more time to focus on the tasks before us. We were fortunate to be at a stage in our lives where we did not have many other commitments. No children, no mortgages to pay. For us, time was more important than money. These two factors always seem to trade against each other.

Understanding the resource at your disposal can be a dispiriting exercise. The temptation is to always compare your own set-up to the competition, who seem to have all the resources you wish you had. Don't resist this temptation, just try to make the comparison analytically. Yes, against us the national teams each had a team of mechanics, but what advantage or disadvantage did that create for them? What would each mechanic do, and how hard are those skills to learn, given some time and energy?

The key to winning at Top Trumps is to make the most of the attributes you have. Maximise the positive effect of your strengths and minimise the negative effect of your weaknesses. In the game you can only play the cards you have been dealt. Fortunately in real life you can work on those attributes to bring your scores up. I am currently working on my washing-up score.

11

Building a team

How long does it take 23 men to change four wheels on a car?

No, it's not a joke. The answer, at least for a Formula One team, is less than two seconds. Indeed, there is even a specific world record for a Formula One pit stop, held (at the time of writing) by the Red Bull Racing team for a 1.88 seconds change on Max Verstappen's car at the 2019 German Grand Prix.

The pit stop is part of a pre-planned race strategy. It is a moment of tension and drama because a hard-won race position can be squandered by a poor change. It works like this. One lap in advance, sometimes much less, the driver is notified via his radio of an impending stop. He comes into the pit lane at full race speed but quickly brings the car down to the pit lane speed limit of 80 km/h. At the team's garage a man holds up a carbon fibre lollipop sign to show the driver where to stop his car. It is critical that the driver hits that mark precisely so that the waiting pit crew do not have to drag their equipment to another position. When the car stops the driver puts the engine into neutral and puts his foot on the brake to stop the wheels spinning as they are changed. Front and rear jack men slide their jacks under the car and lift it 50 millimetres from the track. Three men are crouching ready at each wheel position. The gun man has a powerful compressed air-driven gun that undoes the single-locking nut on each wheel. The 'wheel-off' man pulls the wheel off and the 'wheel-on' man pushes the replacement on to the car. The gun man then tightens up the nut, hits a button to confirm he has completed the job and the car is given the green light to accelerate away. From the moment the car stops, this process takes less than two seconds.

A good pit stop is speedy and safe, but consistency is also important. Depending on the weather, in some Grand Prix races a car might stop up to 10 times. Every time it has to be quick and faultless. Fifty years ago, the average pit stop took over a minute. Technological advancements have played a big role in speeding up the process – car components and tools are designed specifically for the job. Another factor has been the division of labour. The whole task of changing four wheels has been broken down into many specific sub-tasks and a crew member assigned to each. Then the team is brought together to act as one. There is no hierarchy; everyone is equally important, including the driver, whose role is to deliver the car to the crew, keep the brakes on and not stall the engine. Formula One teams now practise pit stops thousands of times so that the task becomes like second nature. Crew members talk of how a good change can feel like it is going in slow motion because it has a kind of effortless flow.

The lesson we can draw from this is that in a high-performing team everyone understands their role, and every role is important. In our team, we saw that this operated on two levels. Firstly, in the race. Secondly, in the preparation for the race.

How we worked together in the race was relatively simple. We were only interested in getting that third man across the finish line as quickly as possible, so we devised a strategy that we believed would achieve that goal. That meant every member of the team delivering their maximum power without the quartet disintegrating. There would be no point in, say, Charlie going out as hard as he possibly could and riding at a pace that is not collectively sustainable for four kilometres. To maintain an efficient aerodynamic form, the second, third and fourth riders have to ride with their front wheel only a few centimetres behind the man in front. If a rider lets a gap open, the benefit of riding behind someone else is significantly reduced and the following rider has to make an unnecessary effort to close the gap, wasting that precious and finite energy. When the team is riding at a pace that is on the limits of their ability, a three-metre gap can be impossible to close. The rider behind will turn himself inside out but still see the team pulling away. If this happens when the team is already down to three, it is nothing short of a disaster. The third man loses contact with the team, slows down dramatically and even if he can keep going to the line, the pace will never be high enough to win.

Our strategy for a race was to use each rider's power most effectively. It came back to the same question – how to finish with three riders who have all completely emptied their anaerobic tank and wasted no energy in the process. Because we each had different strengths and weaknesses, we could all contribute different things to the pace. I had the best strength from a dead start, so I led the team away from the start and got us up to cruising speed. Then, as discussed, Jonny took over for the next five laps. He did his five- to six-lap turn on the front, while I was recovering a little bit on the back, if recovering is possible when you're travelling at over 65 kilometres per hour. Having done his turn, Jonny would swing off, high up on to the banking and leave the race. From then on, Charlie and I usually did one turn each of four laps. Tipper, being the weakest of the team, is protected. He stays in the line for as much as possible, usually only doing one half-lap turn at the front.

This was the basic formula. It could then be adapted to how strongly different riders are riding (which we would know from training session measurements). For example, if Tipper is in the form of his life, we would give him a longer turn on the front. Having agreed to follow a certain strategy, with little room for error or mid-race changes, once in the race it is the responsibility of each member of the team to actually do so. But that's not to say things cannot change. Cyclists often talk about how their legs feel. Sometimes, for no obvious reason, you seem to be working harder to maintain the required pace. The effort accumulates in your legs quicker than usual and you realise that riding to the agreed strategy is going to be unsustainable.

When you hit the front of the line, you have responsibility for setting and maintaining the agreed pace. Go too fast too soon and you will spend longer on the front than the plan dictated. The riders behind you are having to do more work than planned, so are unlikely to be able to ride their same planned turn length because they will have used some of their finite energy tank to accelerate whilst in the wheels. Go too slowly and you will give your team-mates a Herculean task to re-accelerate and claw back the lost time. So you have to make a judgement call about how long to stay on the front. The rider in second place, if they are feeling good, will be itching for you to swing over so they can get on the front and empty their tank. If they are feeling below par, they will be dreading that same moment.

The team pursuit represents a curious kind of teamwork. We inflict pain on each other, and on ourselves, yet at the same time we are protective of one another. In a national team they have so many Top Trump cards that the coaches can select four well-matched riders. There will be only small discrepancies between their performance levels so they do not have to devise strategies to protect their weakest rider, as we do. I would argue, however, that this is a weakness in itself. When those four well-matched riders get on the track, if one of them is having an off day, the team will not have thought through how to manage that situation. Sticking rigidly to the plan is no use if the team explodes before the finish, so I feel it's important to recognise those individual differences, and even use them the best you can.

In March 2017 the four of us moved into a house in Derby. The mundane household tasks like washing-up became part of our preparation for races. Just as we had a rota for who pumped up tyres and mixed energy drinks at races, so we also had a rota for the household chores. An athlete's home life has to be calm, ordered and restful. Disagreements about putting the bins out, or cooking dinner, are a waste of energy. The same applies to the administrative aspects of running the team. Ellie enjoyed booking the travel and accommodation, and we knew we could trust her to get it right, so she took on that role whenever it was required. By playing to individuals' strengths we ensured that everyone felt valued. People are happier when they are doing something they are good at. We all understood that every task contributes to the single aim – going faster on the track. And because victory is shared, the glory is shared. Everyone is equally motivated.

On the track, communication within the team is near impossible. At home, it is essential. Part of our plan to address any issues was to have a weekly meeting at the house, where everyone got a chance to air their worries, concerns, problems, dirty laundry. Sometimes these meetings generated a lot of heated debate. When you have a natural optimist (me) and a natural pessimist (Tipper) in the same unit, differences of opinion are going to occur. Frequently the other members of the team challenged me on my use of data. They challenged my faith in the numbers and my interpretation of them, and though it often upset me, I knew I had to take on these challenges and respond constructively. I knew even just listening to these complaints would make us stronger as a team, and would ensure my own thinking did not become complacent, as well as objectively helping our performance.

The key lesson, as I went through the reverse engineering process, was that as soon as I began to assess the resource at our disposal, a team emerged. They were not yet acting like a team, but

I knew that if I could build them into an effective team around a shared objective, that resource would become a great deal stronger. In other words, resource can become more than the sum of its parts.

Next, I had to get down to work with the team. We had broken down the challenge. Now we had to begin building it back up again, setting specific goals and, above all, measuring. Always measuring.

Part 4

Develop your tools

12

Measure what matters

Francesco Moser was one of the leading road racing cyclists of the 1970s and early 1980s. Hailing from the Trentino region of Italy, Moser was world road race champion in 1977, three times Italian champion, and won a host of classic one-day races, including three victories at the notoriously difficult Paris–Roubaix. His tall, broad figure, combined with a smooth pedalling style, was well suited to riding on cobbles, where power is paramount. He excelled at time trials too. Throughout his career he amassed a total of 273 victories on the road.

Moser was approaching the end of his career when he invited the world's cycling press on a trip to Mexico City in January 1984. He had a surprise for them. He was about to take on the Hour Record. This is a record that stands apart from the rest of bike racing. We might call it the blue riband event of track cycling, only it is attempted so infrequently, and in a sense it doesn't really belong to the world of track cycling. The words iconic and legend-ary are overused in cycling, but they fit the Hour Record well. The concept is simple. A rider pedals around a velodrome for one hour and records a distance for that period. If they beat the existing record they become the Hour Record holder. The record's pres-tige is founded upon its brutality. The rider has to calculate then maintain an effort so punishing that they will finish with absolutely nothing remaining, and they have to stay locked into their racing position for the whole hour. Mental strength and resilience plays a huge role. To take on the Hour Record takes a great deal of cour-age. You are announcing to the world that you are better than every cyclist who has gone before you. It is something to win the world championships and beat all of your contemporaries. It is something else to beat every cyclist in history.

There is a long history of attempts – the record dates back to 1876, when American Frank Dodds rode 16.476 miles on a penny-farthing, and many of the greatest riders have attempted it, including Tour de France winners Fausto Coppi and Jacques Anquetil. When Moser began considering a record attempt, the official distance to beat stood at 49.431 kilometres (30.715 miles), set by Belgian Eddy Merckx in 1972 in Mexico City, where the alti-tude of 2,300 metres significantly reduced the air density. Merckx, widely acknowledged to be the greatest racing cyclist in history, proclaimed it the 'hardest ride I have ever done'.

In the summer of 1983, Francesco Moser sat down with his coach and his team manager to discuss the viability of attacking Merckx's record. The distance was impressive but it had been set over a decade before and cycling technology had moved on. Merckx took a specially made track bike to Mexico City, designed to be ultralight and with a riding position identical to that he used in road racing. Aerodynamics were barely considered. Moser's coach, Francesco Conconi, believed that with greater focus on the science of physiology and aerodynamics, Merckx's seemingly unbeatable record was within reach.

A team was brought together and the project was broken down into its constituent parts – training, bike, clothing and logistics. Conconi worked closely with Moser to extend his aerobic threshold, the maximum effort he could sustain for one hour, through specific interval training. Every session was recorded using a heart-rate monitor, something of a novelty at the time. Simultaneously, Moser's team of engineers, led by Antonio Brandazzi, began building a bike that would cut through that low density Mexican air. Brandazzi understood that a light bike was not necessary for a velodrome. Instead, he worked on a position that brought Moser's tall frame into a low crouch, and on a pair of wheels over which the air would flow smoothly. Italian manufacturer Ambrosio developed for Moser the world's first disc wheel. This 'filled' wheel had a solid surface on both sides. No spokes were visible. They were heavy, but Brandazzi reasoned that their weight was an advantage. They would act as flywheels, helping Moser to maintain his speed. This has been an ongoing point of contention for those attempting the Hour Record and their experts. My view is that high inertia wheels are not of much benefit. The inertial energy stored in wheels is relatively small when compared to the kinetic energy stored in the rider's mass.

The silver bike that Moser climbed on to on 19 January 1984 was nearly twice as heavy as Merckx's machine and looked outlandish by contemporary standards. Moser wore a silk skinsuit, a Lycra hat stretched over his head and aero shoe covers pulled over strapless shoes. The sun was shining as a vociferous crowd filled the old Olympic Velodrome.

Moser's approach was cautious. He declared that if he clocked times close to Merckx's 5km, 10km and 20km splits, he would keep going to the full hour. If not, he would pull out and try again another day. Not only was he faster than the Belgian at these early markers, Moser was faster throughout the 60 minutes. He became the first rider in history to break the 50km mark, racking up 50.808km. Four days later he went again and this time extended the record to 51.151km. This was a seminal moment in the history of the Hour Record. No longer could a strong road rider do a few weeks of extra training and turn up at a velodrome, hoping his legs would be good enough to steal beyond the record. Now the Hour Record became a specialist event in itself, and anyone considering it had to be prepared to invest considerable time and energy beforehand. Cutting-edge equipment had become essential. Moser's record stood for almost a decade, before another flurry of attempts took place in the mid-nineties. Technology, and sports science, had moved on again.

Francesco Moser's Hour Record was a pivotal moment in the history of aerodynamics in cycling. Naturally, the traditionalist world of cycling took a while to catch up with the Italian's innovations. Some of the more forward-thinking riders began using disc wheels in road time trials. And then in 1989 the American Greg LeMond won the Tour de France by just eight seconds, beating Frenchman Laurent Fignon in a time trial into Paris. LeMond used a rear disc wheel, an aero helmet and handlebar extensions (called tri-bars at the time because they had been pioneered in triathlon, a new sport that had a healthy attitude to innovation). These extensions, which are now used by practically every time triallist, triathlete and pursuit racer around the world, gave LeMond a lower, narrower and more compact position which was more aerodynamic and did not compromise how much power he could put through the pedals. Fignon had got the memo about disc wheels but not about aero extensions or aero helmets. He rode bare-headed, his trademark blond ponytail flapping in the wind as he desperately tried to save his yellow jersey on the Champs-Elysees in Paris. When Fignon crossed the line and collapsed in defeat, the cycling world saw that aerodynamic technology, wisely used, could win bike races.

If you are an amateur racing cyclist with a little spare cash, or a shiny new credit card, you could go out today and buy a flashy new pair of wheels. Your assumption might be that those wheels will help you to go faster because they are more aerodynamic. This is free speed, in the sense of no additional physical effort required (let's not worry about the credit card bill). But assuming is not good enough. How will you *know* that these wheels make you go faster? For that matter, how do you *know* anything about sporting performance?

Measurement is critical to modern elite sport. If you can't measure it, you can't improve it. Intuition has a place – after all, athletes are human beings, not robots – but if something can be measured, you should at least consider measuring it. The important thing is to focus on those variables that will count, those that will make a meaningful difference to your performance. None of us has unlimited time, energy and money, so measuring and analysing every variable is not pragmatic. Find the measures that matter, then record them over time.

For a team pursuit squad in cycling there are two measures that really matter – power and drag coefficient (CdA). Power represents the energy the rider is transferring from his body into the bike, and therefore into forward motion. CdA is a measure of how aerodynamic the rider and his bike are. The two factors that make up CdA are frontal area (A) and Cd (drag coefficient), which is a dimensionless value that quantifies the drag experienced by an object. The higher the speed, the more impact the CdA has on performance because aerodynamic drag power varies cubically to velocity, and therefore the faster you go the larger proportion of your input power goes to aero drag. If Francesco Moser had adopted a standard road racing position on his bike, and worn a loose jersey, perhaps he would not have broken Merckx's record.

But that's very specific to professional cycling... let's get back to our amateur rider and that shiny new pair of wheels. The best way to assess whether or not they will help them to go faster is to use what is commonly known as the scientific method. One of the cornerstones of modern science, the scientific method is used across all scientific disciplines. It is central to the development of scientific theories and is also used in empirical sciences such as social science. The model is that the scientist starts with a hypothesis, then he or she designs and conducts an experiment to test the hypothesis, collects the results, compares them to the expected results and then modifies the hypothesis. The scientist keeps following this process until the results are consistent and he or she has enough data to explain the conclusions.

To test how aerodynamic a new pair of wheels are, or any other piece of kit, is a straightforward process. The experiment has already been designed, so you would simply book in at a wind tunnel or a velodrome and run some controlled tests that compare old versus new.

I admit that very few amateur cyclists are going to take themselves to a wind tunnel to test their kit. Most will simply accept the claims of the manufacturer. The point, though, is that measurement requires a scientific approach. Measurement requires data. Collecting data can be a time-consuming business, which is why selecting the measures that matter is so important. Focus on what will make a difference, then really develop your understanding of it.

Only once you have an understanding of the measures that matter, and some robust data that gives you some direction, can you begin to add in further measures. In most of our training sessions we measure air speed (which shows how well you're drafting the rider in front), wheel speed and power, as well as utilising 3-axis accelerometer and gyroscope data to imply tyre forces, the position of the bike on the track and the angle of the bike versus the track. When I am not riding my bike, I have my head stuck in a spreadsheet, looking at the data, looking for cause and effect. How does the angle of the bike on the track affect wheel speed and centre of mass speed? How does the width and profile of a tyre affect rolling resistance and control? How does the efficiency of drafting vary with different rider orders and pacing strategies? When I am trying to find correlations like this I start from a hypothesis, often framed as a question, then run a series of tests to assess that hypothesis. Usually these tests are on the velodrome, but when testing equipment, we sometimes have to design and build a testing rig. Given unlimited time and resources we could theoretically run so many tests that we understand precisely how every minute factor affects performance. Instead we focus on those we believe have the most impact and make judgements on the rest based on whatever evidence others have collected.

Faced with any new scenario I will start out with a hypothesis about which factors affect performance, and through measurement I can refine that list of factors. The resulting list, ordered from most impactful to least, defines how we prioritise our time, effort and money. This is just the same prioritisation process that many people in a demanding job will go through – first, tick off the jobs that will make the most difference to your performance, then if any time remains, keep working your way down the list.

It is too easy to get sucked into a way of thinking that says money will easily solve every problem, and conversely that lack of money means failure is guaranteed. From my own experience, this mentality is present in track cycling too (and is probably in all sports involving technology); the success of British Cycling, supported by their enormous UK Sport funding, accentuated it. It is simply not true. There might be a minimum level of budget required to be part of the competition, but beyond that the relationship between money and performance is not a linear correlation. What makes more difference is attitude, and measurement is central to this.

Training regimes do not vary so much between teams. Everyone knows the basics of what makes a good pursuit rider and everyone knows the different types of training that can improve performance. Typically this is a blend of long rides on the road for endurance, gym work for strength and intense track sessions for anaerobic capacity. If every team are cognisant of this basic structure, what makes the difference between winning and losing is the detail. You can only know how the detail affects performance by measuring it.

From what I have learnt, measurement must always relate back to our goals. In the mid 1970s a young computer engineer called John Doerr went to work at Intel, then a fledgling computer processing company based in Santa Clara, California. There, Doerr worked for a man called Andy Groves, a Hungarian immigrant who has become known as the father of management science. Groves was an inspiring leader and teacher, and under his impetus, Intel became the force behind the rapid expansion of home computers in the United States. During his time at the company, Intel's revenues increased from $1.9bn to $26bn. Groves advocated a new way to achieving results, which he called Objectives and Key Results (OKRs). To use the OKR method is to set an Objective, then specify a small number of Key Results that will lead you to achieve that objective. The key results have to be measurable and relatively simple. Ideally when reviewing whether you achieved your results you would be able to answer yes or no. An objective can be long- or short-term, and regular reviews (in a corporate environment these are usually done quarterly; in our case they are done weekly) are part of the process.

At Intel, one of the side effects of OKRs was to democratise the workplace. Achievement became defined by what someone executed rather than their ideas, their job title or their career experience. Employees were valued based on what they achieved. OKRs were not, however, linked to financial compensation. This was because Groves believed that an objective had to have a stronger underlying reason than financial gain. Of course, if you achieved all your objectives, you probably had a pretty strong argument for a pay rise...

Doerr took Groves' OKR framework and ran with it. After leaving Intel in 1980, Doerr worked as a venture capitalist, providing backing for many entrepreneurs, particularly in the technology sector. In 1999 Doerr went to meet Google founders Larry Page and Sergey Brin. At that time Google had minimal funding and was still a beta (test status) search engine. Page and Brin were working in a garage, and Doerr did his presentation to them on a ping-pong table. As well as pitching investment to them, Doerr pitched the idea of OKRs as a way of managing the company. Some articles about that now-legendary meeting have said that Page and Brin loved the idea of OKRs. Doerr himself, however, in a 2018 TED Talk, said that Brin merely said, 'We don't have any other way to manage this company so we'll give it a go.'

It went pretty well. Much of Google's growth, and that of other tech companies such as Netflix and Amazon, can be attributed to OKRs. Now, Google still uses Groves' method. Each quarter every Google employee has to write down their objectives and key results. The framework is applicable to any form of objective, work or personal. Rather like the scientific method, its beauty lies in its simplicity. The focus on measurement gives you direction. And whether or not you choose to use OKRs as a way of framing your objectives, it is useful to remember this: measure what matters, and you are on the right path to achieving results.

13

Create positive feedback loops

Once you know which measures matter, it is then time to refine the methodology, and accuracy is paramount. What we want to create are positive feedback loops – a system where one variable increases the quality of another variable, which in turn further increases the quality of the first variable. Some have also called this a virtuous circle, the opposite of a vicious circle.

Positive feedback loops use measurement to create a culture of continual improvement. Without them we would just be working with the same information, coming up with the same conclusions and never getting any deeper knowledge about our performance.

Human beings are fundamentally set up to use positive feedback loops. Indeed, our evolution has been based on them. Over millennia, humans have taken on information from a wide variety of sources and adapted their behaviour accordingly. Information:

a tiger ate my friend. Behaviour adaptation: avoid tigers. That is how the fittest have survived, by learning as they go along, by using feedback, then seeking more feedback.

Now, we are more concerned with improving our health than dodging wild animals that might eat us. With technology gathering pace in recent years, we all now have access to far more information. Wearable technology, for example, gives us a wealth of data about how much physical activity we are doing and the quality of our sleep. Millions of people own a smart watch and have access to this sort of data. But improvements in their exercise routine or sleep patterns will only come through actively using the data rather than passively absorbing it. This process does not need to be overly complicated. Simply, it is about understanding where you are, identifying ways to get better, then using the data to track that progress. Then repeating the process. Positive feedback loops happen unconsciously. Used consciously they are powerful tools to making performance gains.

Positive feedback loops are constructed of stages that together make up a continuous cycle. The scientific method described in the last chapter is a good example of a positive feedback loop. In principle there are five stages:

1. **Plan.** Every feedback loop must start with a clear plan. This will outline the objectives of the project, but just as important is that the plan includes the methodology and metrics to be used.
2. **Collect information.** If we want to change something, we have to find a way to measure it. Through

testing (either in a live or a simulated environment) we can collect data about how our initiatives are performing. Measures must lead to actions. The smart watch example is pertinent here – a watch can track a person's heart rate through the day, but without an understanding of physiology and a specific goal to aim at, the data is not very helpful.

3. **Analyse.** Here we are looking for the data to show us cause and effect.

4. **Discuss and reflect.** Analysis will not always quickly yield clear results. Sometimes the picture can be confusing. This is where working in a cross-discipline team can bring different perspectives and fresh insights. And sometimes the thought process needs time for discussion and reflection. I find some of my best ideas come not when I am staring at a laptop but when I am out riding my bike.

5. **Adjust the course.** Having established cause and effect, we can begin to take decisions about our behaviour, or at least develop our hypothesis. Early in the process, we are more likely to focus on improving the richness of the data. If the first iteration of the cycle has given no clear results we need to ask why, then alter the focus of stages one to four.

Positive feedback loops are firmly embedded in how many industries and professions operate. In marketing, for example, it is essential to understand how a campaign is being received by its target audience; otherwise a company risks shouting about itself into a void and wasting a lot of money, or worse – generating negative publicity. An effective marketing campaign will not only have measures and metrics built into its plan, it will also have a variety of tools to analyse the data and adjust the channels being used. Increasingly the technology to manage these loops is automated and operates with minimal human supervision.

In 2019 I began working with a start-up technology company called Notio. Founded as part of the development of a futuristic concept bike in 2016 by Canadian bike manufacturers Argon 18, Notio have created a sensor for bikes that measures a whole range of variables. Their sensor, which is little more than a small black box you attach to your handlebars, would not have been viable 10 years ago because the several different sensors it houses were too bulky. Now, both the size and the cost of the sensors has come down.

What Notio have achieved is to create the technology to enable accurate, precise and repeatable aerodynamic testing in the real world, making aerodynamic measurement available to any rider. This democratises aerodynamics, enabling those who have previously been unable to access expensive technology to make a step into the world of aerodynamics. Now, riders of any level can get faster without having to find more power. The sensor collects and processes information every 20 milliseconds, sends it to an app and the data can later be uploaded to analytical software. For a rider engaged in high-speed bike racing against the clock – pursuiting, time trialling or triathlon – aerodynamic drag is by far the biggest proportion of energy loss. All the energy a rider produces has to go somewhere (coming back to the first principles of physics, energy cannot be destroyed) and up to 80 per cent of that energy goes in riding through the air.

To get to an accurate CdA figure, the sensor works on the principle that if it can measure all the various other ways that energy is lost during cycling, the balance must be aerodynamic drag, which can then be normalised and expressed as a CdA value. The sensor measures air speed, slope, vibration and air density, and using these measured variables, along with user-defined variables, it can then calculate the rider's CdA and send this to the rider in real time as well as logging all the data for analysis later.

Wout van Aert is a prodigiously talented professional bike rider. A triple world cyclo-cross champion, in 2019 Van Aert was beginning to turn his focus to road racing. As well as aiming to do well in the tough one-day classics such as Paris–Roubaix, in which the riders hurl themselves along cobbled farm tracks, Van Aert also set his sights on improving his time trialling. His coaches had correctly identified that the young Belgian could be good at time trials because of his ability to sustain a world-class power output for 30 to 70 minutes. Cyclo-cross racing is a winter discipline which takes place on short off-road circuits, often very muddy. Races last for one hour. The riders go hard from the start, and keep that effort going to the finish. It is therefore unsurprising that the cyclo-cross world champion has some of the best power numbers in the sport.

In the spring of 2019 Van Aert was in good physical shape but needed to improve his aerodynamics. His team, Jumbo-Visma, asked for my help. However, Van Aert's schedule did not allow for a visit to a wind tunnel. In fact, his only gap in a busy racing programme was while he was at an altitude training camp in the Alps, a long way from the nearest wind tunnel. I flew out to the training camp and talked to Van Aert and his coaches about what we would need to run some accurate tests. Understandably they were keen to minimise Wout's stress and exertion levels; altitude training camps are tough enough already, without having to do full-speed time-trial efforts just so an aerodynamics geek can populate his spreadsheets.

We needed to find a location where we could perform consistent and repeatable tests. After scouting around the area we found a four-kilometre section of road with a slight gradient of 4 per cent. The road surface was good, there were no obstructions and traffic was sparse. Not many people want to visit a ski resort in May. The gradient meant that Wout could ride downhill at a speed close to his flat time-trial speed, but with considerably less effort. The team set up a car at the bottom of the hill to bring Wout back up to the start, and had a mechanic at the top of the hill to adjust his bike as required.

With the Notio sensors attached, we ran 15 tests, trying out different positions on the bike. Because the conditions were uncomplicated and repeatable, and because Wout was able to ride very fast, we pulled together a clean and comprehensive data set, which led to some clear conclusions, and some actions for the team to take.

A few weeks later, to the surprise of many commentators, Van Aert won the time trial at the Critérium du Dauphiné, an important warm-up race for the Tour de France. A week later he demonstrated that the Dauphiné result was no fluke by winning the Belgian time-trial championship, beating Victor Campenaerts, the holder of the Hour Record.

Wout's objectives moved on. As a multi-talented professional rider, his team place many – sometimes conflicting – demands upon him. Yet if we had continued the process of time-trial testing, and perhaps widened the analysis to examine other aspects of his performance, he would have kept improving.

I used Notio sensors on all the Team KGF bikes for every training session on the track. We logged the data every half lap and developed our own analysis software that utilised all the unique variables that Notio collects. This enabled us to create our own metrics and presentation of performance data, of which we have built up a solid database, the bedrock of everything we did. It could be construed as rather frustrating, or even boring, that a sporting event is so defined by data, numbers, maths and physics, because we still like to think of sport in terms of the Olympic ideals, of talented amateurs competing on instinct. In reality, though, the sporting world is a long way from that. Perhaps Eddy Merckx's generation was the last to compete in that way; science took hold of sport in the late twentieth century and has accelerated exponentially in the age of the internet. As an engineer and a professional sportsperson it is my job to understand precisely what shapes performance. Superstition has no place in that process. Innovation and mathematics do. Where science and analysis exists, we should use it. Where it does not exist, we should try to create it.

At the Mercedes AMG Petronas team, the cars are rigged to provide some 16,000 channels of data. This data provides the team engineers with information on every aspect of the car's performance and allows them to isolate individual components or features. Take the pit-stop strategy as an example of how the team approach measurement: first, the team developed a strategy for the pit stops based on experience and a hefty dose of idealism. Second, the team created sensors to measure the key parameters of that strategy. They decided on which measures mattered. Then, having started doing practice sessions, they began to see the gaps in their analysis – all the parts of the pit stop that they were not measuring. So they developed more sensors, absorbed more data and improved the performance.

Earlier we took the pit stop as an example of great teamwork. Now we can see that focused, thought-through measurement is another reason that a team can change four tyres in less than two seconds. But the gun man crouching in position, ready to loosen a single wheel locking nut, has not only practised his task thousands of times, he has also done so with many sensors attached to his gun. Those sensors measure at what angle he connects with the gun to the nut, how long the nut takes to release its torque, how long it takes for the tyre to come off, and so on... every fraction of a second in that process can be analysed and optimised, such as changing the shape of the nut to allow quicker engagement of the gun, or deciding where the gunman needs to focus his gaze as the car rolls in. In measuring to this minute level of detail, the team are gathering rich data and a positive feedback loop that fuels continuous improvement. They have the budget to do so, and they understand that success in modern Formula One comes from aggregating thousands of fractional gains.

If most people or organisations would write down a handful of key results for each objective, a Formula One engineer would probably write down a hundred. But the principle is still the same – decide what will drive better performance and measure it.

Most of us do not have the resources to follow the Formula One approach. But if you have taken some time to decide which measures matter, take a little more time to consider the richness of the data. Is there a feedback loop in place? Can its accuracy be improved? Or its frequency? Does correlating two variables give you a new insight? If a certain metric is not improving over time (when you had planned for it to do so) does that mean some of your assumptions are wrong?

Data is organic. It changes as we change. It is objective and honest. Best of all, if properly used, it guides us towards improvement.

Part 5

Set the plan in motion

14

Control your environment

To begin seriously pursuing our goals I knew we had to build an environment in the UK that was conducive to high performance. We needed the right training facilities, and that meant access to a velodrome, a gym and some good training roads. Derby is well positioned in this last regard because you can head north into the Peak District if you feel the need to throw yourself at some steep hills, or you can head south for a flatter landscape. Derby's central location, close to the M1, makes it easy to get to road-racing and time-trial events up and down the country.

A central part of everyone in the team committing to the project was that we had agreed to live together for a year. It was important that we were all on a level playing field and could spend time together, not just undertake training sessions then disperse. For Charlie this was a significant upheaval because he had to transfer his engineering degree from the University of Teesside to the

University of Derby. For all of us there was a feeling of putting our lives on hold, and though I was optimistic about our chances of achieving our goals, there was always a nagging doubt in the back of my mind as to how sustainable this was. But once the ball started rolling, these worries disappeared and I just lived in the moment. Looking back now, it wasn't sustainable, but we made it work.

Most of our training was to take place in the Derby velodrome, so it made sense for us to live as close as possible. Fortunately for us, the area surrounding Derby velodrome is one of the cheapest in the city. Still, we didn't have much money, and estate agents are usually quite allergic to renting houses to four lads in their twenties. So we found a creative solution. Jonny and I took a trip to the estate agent's office and walked in holding hands. We told the agent that the house was just for us and Jonny looked lovingly into my eyes (we had created a whole backstory for our relationship that sadly we never got to reveal). It was very hard to hold it together, especially when Jonny fluttered his eyelashes at me. Documents signed, we escaped that office as quickly as we could and made sure we got round the corner before collapsing in laughter.

The house on Portland Street was a 1930s semi-detached with three bedrooms. It was too small for the four of us, but it was all we could afford. Mostly it was Tipper who slept on the sofa. We installed a curtain down the middle of the lounge so Tipper had some 'bedroom privacy'. Charlie's room was so small that his head and feet touched opposite walls when he lay on his mattress, which of course lay on the floor without a bed frame as there was bike kit everywhere. There always seemed to be at least one room blocked by a stationary trainer. One of the reasons we chose the house was its lock-up garage that could comfortably house all our bikes. Before we moved in it had not occurred to us that living in the highest crime area in the highest crime town in the Midlands, with a garage full of expensive bikes, could be a problem. It did not take very long for the local thieves to notice our presence.

* * *

Unless you are an elite racing cyclist, or starring in a film that requires a Martian landscape, you've probably never been to the top of Mount Teide in Tenerife. It is a strange place – isolated and bleak. An active volcano, Spain's highest peak has a ribbon of beautifully surfaced road running across a lunar landscape, making it the perfect place for high altitude training in the sun. Hang around for long enough and you'll inevitably see a pack of skinny young people smoothly pedalling bicycles that cost more than the average family car. Up there, at 2,400 metres above sea level, a professional endurance athlete can improve oxygen uptake efficiency by applying a novel and unique stimulus that is hard to replicate anywhere else, and one that results in great physiological adaptations.

The benefits of altitude training are well proven. We just had to find a way to get access to the benefits, on a much lower budget than our rivals. After access to training facilities, athletes need good nutrition and plenty of rest. Luxury hotels are exactly that – a luxury.

Our altitude training camps on Mount Teide were designed to familiarise us with altitude, both from a physiological perspective and from a psychological perspective. So much of performance is in

your head. Knowing what the sensations of altitude are like is criti-
cal to performing at sea level. Two weeks of training, resting, eating,
analysing. Repetitive, sometimes boring, but my team-mates were
my closest friends and that made it a lot easier. Sometimes it could
all feel rather surreal – riding up and down the same stretch of
mountain road in the blazing sun, halfway up a volcano, brutalising
my own body. At times like that I had to keep reminding myself of
the connection between this situation and the four minutes of pain
I would be experiencing at a World Cup.

Our training camps were a bit different to those run by the big
professional teams. They had nice hotels, their own chefs, mechan-
ics, masseurs, physiotherapists. We funded the camps ourselves
on credit cards, staying in the cheapest Airbnb properties on the
mountain. The place was halfway up the mountain and completely
off-grid. Electricity is supplied by a cranky petrol generator. Water
comes from a rainwater tank on the roof. The only heat is from a log
fire. For the duration of our stay we were our own cooks, mechan-
ics, physios and coaches. And because there aren't enough beds in
the house, we rented a wrecked old motorhome and parked it on
the drive. This was a *Breaking Bad* training camp.

Living together, trying to keep on top of the housework, shiv-
ering under blankets on top of a mountain in Tenerife – all of this
brought the team together. We always figured out a way through, and
that made our friendship stronger. There were stressful moments,
and many heated debates, sometimes about aerodynamic drag
coefficients, sometimes about the washing machine. But there were
many more moments of fun and laughter. We became a compact

and strong unit. That would not have happened if we had all lived separately and only met up for training sessions.

* * *

Beyond controlling a physical environment, it is crucial to consider the other factors that can affect performance, in particular the factors that affect our daily habits. An athlete's performance is built on continual tiny increments. There are no great leaps forward. And an athlete's daily existence can be boring, revolving as it does around training, eating and resting. It can be easy to slip into bad habits – the occasional chocolate bar, or staying up too late to watch a film. All our habits add up. The aim is to cut out those habits that negatively affect performance, and keep the habits that positively affect performance.

To do this I have always been mindful that I need to control my social environment. Tipper, Charlie and Jonny were the perfect group to be part of because we exerted a positive peer influence on each other. It gave me the incentive to push harder for better self-control. Every athlete knows what they *should* be doing – the question is whether they have the self-discipline to consistently behave according to that model.

One negative behaviour among elite athletes is over-training – when you go beyond your training programme, thinking that doing more equates to getting even better than planned. Inevitably, what follows is exhaustion – physical and mental – and underperformance. Rather like throwing money at a problem, simply doing more training does not necessarily lead to increased performance.

Tipper, Jonny, Charlie and I had our moments of being competitive young lads and trying to rip each other's legs off, but most of the time we understood that would be counter-productive. We were a team and our collective performance depended on each of us religiously following our training plans.

I have always tried to think holistically about the factors that influence my performance. Training, sleep and nutrition are the obvious ones. But there are other less obvious factors – what books and magazines should I read? What are the air pollution levels where I live? Which of my friends and family are most supportive of what I am doing?

The principle of controlling one's environment applies to any endeavour. Reverse engineering dictates that we set plans to bridge a performance gap. The environment we operate in plays a significant role in determining our chances of successfully implementing that plan. The more we can control that environment, the firmer the foundations on which we build.

15

Bring people with you

In the run-up to the 2008 Beijing Olympics, Chris Boardman was busy being a Secret Squirrel. The group were working hard to develop new equipment and improving aerodynamics was top of their agenda. Another key member of the team was Rob Lewis, an aerodynamicist who also had the great advantage of knowing nothing about cycling. Lewis, Boardman and their colleagues were working in a wind tunnel, testing new ideas. Because bringing squad riders to the wind tunnel was expensive and time-consuming they had a couple of regulars – Olympians Jason Queally and Rob Hayles – on whom they ran tests. The not unreasonable assumption was that the Secret Squirrel Club could develop pieces of kit with Queally and Hayles, then roll them out to the other riders at races.

In late 2007 much of the focus was on helmets, an area where the team thought big gains could be made. For the pursuit events the riders already had aero helmets that performed well – as long as the rider kept their head straight and facing forward. But for the sprint events no one had ever really considered aerodynamics. Partly this was because it was a more complex problem. In a sprint race or a keirin the rider is constantly moving their head around to check their opponents' position. The riders' speed in such races is hugely variable, and the periods of time involved are so short that it is difficult to achieve accurate testing based on consistent data. The solution they came up with was a compromise between aerodynamics and practicality, much more rounded at the back of the head than a standard aero helmet and with a tinted visor over the eyes (it's important to look mean and moody in the sprint events).

In his autobiography, *Triumphs and Turbulence*, Boardman relates how he brought some prototypes of the new helmet to the track in Manchester to show the coaches and the rest of the riders. To achieve both aerodynamic efficiency and to meet safety standards the Secret Squirrels had opted to use carbon fibre in their construction. This made the prototypes heavier than the standard issue helmets the riders were used to, something they voiced concern about.

Here we can draw a line all the way back to Francesco Moser and Eddy Merckx. Moser's engineers understood that on a velodrome aerodynamics were far more important than weight, in a way that Merckx's engineers did not. And even in 2008, over 20 years after Moser's Hour Record, here was a group of track riders worrying about weight over aerodynamics. The culture of saving weight is deeply ingrained in cyclists because in road racing it does matter, and most cyclists start their careers in road racing, even if they later switch to another discipline. Also, perhaps, weight-saving is an easier concept to get your head around. Anyone who goes up a hill on a bicycle wishes they were dragging up fewer kilograms. It is easy to pick up a bike and feel how heavy it is, compared to picking up a bike and feeling how aerodynamic it is. Weight means nothing on the track.

In February 2008 the Great Britain team travelled to Copenhagen for a round of the World Cup. Boardman went along and took the new helmets with him, along with various other pieces of new kit that the Secret Squirrel Club had been testing. He was astonished, and frustrated, to find that only one in five of the team's riders actually used the new kit that he had spent so many hours researching and building. It must have felt like a slap in the face. But then Boardman noticed that the riders who had adopted the new kit, and ridden in the new positions, were those that had played a part in the testing process. They had seen the work that had gone into the new kit, the science behind it and the theoretical improvements to performance it delivered. In other words, they believed in it.

On returning from Denmark, Boardman arranged for the whole team to come to the wind tunnel facility and go through a series of tests in which they could try different pieces of kit and see the benefits for themselves. While they pedalled, live data was projected on to the floor in front of them. To deliver the message with maximum impact, the data was shown as seconds saved or lost. In this way the riders could see with their own eyes the rewards on offer. After that session, every rider in the team adopted at least some of the new kit and advice. And we know what happened in Beijing

– Great Britain was the dominant nation on the track, winning 12 gold medals.

What is the lesson in this story? We have already established that a high-performing team is composed of individuals who know their roles and are committed to working collectively to improve performance – think back to the Formula One pit stop that takes less than two seconds. The individuals in these teams are highly motivated to improve their performance because they understand what they are doing, why they are doing it, and what levers they possess to improve their performance. In other words, they are empowered. The riders that Boardman employed in the testing process were empowered, albeit almost accidentally, because they saw at first hand the outcomes of the testing. Once he got the rest of the team into the wind tunnel, they became empowered too.

Everyone in the Great Britain team at that time bought into a common philosophy – that using science to challenge older methods would yield more speed and ultimately more Olympic medals. Some of the riders may have chosen not to adopt certain new developments, but at least they were doing so equipped with the facts on both sides of the argument. Too often in my sport, and many others, the system is designed to impart knowledge in a top-down way. A performance director outlines a performance strategy, hands that down to the coaches (and in some systems there will be a hierarchy of coaching staff) who translate it into plans for their athletes. The last person in the chain is the athlete. He or she is given a training plan and a set of equipment and told to get on with it. Your job is to pedal the bicycle, not to ask difficult questions. So the athlete has little understanding of the science behind the plans and isn't able to participate in a meaningful discussion about them. This dynamic is accentuated when you have young athletes joining a very established and outwardly impressive programme. Above all, these young athletes want to achieve their goals and impress their coaches. They soon learn that it is best to keep your mouth shut and pedal because challenges to the hierarchy are not taken well. In the end, though, such a culture of fear is counter-productive. It makes the athletes miserable and the coaching staff miss out on the valuable feedback and ideas they could be generating from their athletes, who have to ride the bikes and provide feedback. Would Formula One engineers ignore things the driver had to say? Of course not. They are the primary source of information and their input leads the development, since they are the ones who have to go out and perform.

This point – about listening to people on the ground – is not only applicable to elite sport, but to the wider working world too. Corporate history is littered with examples of major failures that could have been avoided had the companies in question been better at listening to their employees. In 2014 General Motors was forced to recall 14 million cars because of faulty ignition motors. Yet as early as 2005 employees had noticed the underlying causes and escalated their concerns to management. No action was taken until customers began complaining.

The bigger the organisation the bigger the gap between the leaders and the men and women on the ground. Yet finding ways to close that gap, to listen to the people with direct experience of delivering the organisation's proposition is essential. It can avoid costly mistakes and, beyond that, vastly enrich the conversation about how to improve products.

I have always believed in an athlete-centric system in which the athletes are given the tools to understand and improve their own performance. From the start of Team KGF I shared with my team-mates my ideas, hypotheses, test results and what they meant for our approach. Training sessions became blended with science lessons as I talked through the scientific principles and methods I was using. Information was always shared freely within the team, whereas in other systems it is used as some kind of power play, where the coaches believe that holding information close gives them some kind of advantage. For me it was crazy to be in a team and not trust your colleagues.

Much like Boardman inviting the Great Britain riders into the wind tunnel, I gave my team-mates spreadsheets (sometimes simplified to avoid bogging everyone down in data) that showed the benefits of using one helmet over another, or how their performance would change if they put out more power, or less power, or held their head in a better position, so that they knew what to expect and how much impact all of this had on their own performance when race day came around. Equipped with the information, my team-mates felt trusted and empowered. They knew that if they disagreed with something, they could speak up. We had an unspoken agreement that no question or idea was stupid, and everything could be challenged. Everything was up for debate, because in that way we were not shutting down ideas too early. I have faith in myself (the others would probably say blind faith) and I am an eternal optimist, but I was prepared to be challenged. It could become frustrating. When you are tired after training, you don't always feel like explaining a spreadsheet, or running through your assumptions for what feels like the 100th time. But I knew it was important to do these things because it meant that when we lined up on the track for our next race, all four of us would have confidence in the way we had prepared. That in turn means less nerves, less stress and more focus on the job in hand.

The principal difference between Team KGF and other larger teams I encountered was that we were coaching and analysing ourselves. We were investing in ourselves. In a big team the analysis is done by one group of people and the riding is done by another group of people. The two groups interact, but they certainly do not share a house. And they don't always share objectives. An athlete wants to achieve a certain level of performance. A coach wants to protect his or her job, and possibly get promoted. These two objectives are not necessarily aligned. And even if we assume that a coach does want success, it might not be in the same event, to the same timescale or even with the same athlete. For a coach, it is a job. Arguably, this means passions are not as strong as they are for an athlete.

In a hierarchical coaching system, if you want to get promoted, it pays to toe the line and please your boss, even if you disagree with his or her methodology. In Team KGF, analysis and performance were completely united and we benefited from every improvement we could find.

Empowerment and trust are central to high-performing teams. This means that the individuals within a team are trusted and empowered, but the team must also be empowered as a unit. If that team is operating within a hierarchical system, be it a large corporation, an educational or sporting organisation, and it can be given the right level of autonomy, it will thrive. Give a team the resources it needs (or as much as you can afford) and ask them to go and deliver something, and generally speaking that team will rise to the challenge. It is in their interests to do so. People respond positively to being treated like adults. When you treat them like children, they fall into negative patterns of behaviour.

* * *

During the twelfth stage of the 2019 Tour de France, Australian cyclist Rohan Dennis pulled up at the side of the road and climbed off his bike. He travelled to the finish in Bagnères-de-Bigorre by car then disappeared into his team bus. When he emerged, showered and changed, he was accompanied by his agent and refused to say anything to the waiting journalists, who were sensing there was something unusual going on. Leaving the Tour de France midway through the race is common enough, but Dennis seemed to be riding strongly. He had not crashed and did not appear to be sick. Even stranger was the fact that the next day's stage was an individual time trial, the discipline in which Dennis was reigning world champion. He would have been favourite to win.

His team management purported to be as mystified as everyone else, though at the same time reports began to filter through that Dennis had spent much of the stage riding alongside his team car, arguing with his team managers. The team scrambled to respond to the situation, telling the press that they were confused and disappointed and concerned for their rider's welfare. They then launched an 'investigation' into the episode. If the bridge between Dennis and his team had been burning, this was petrol poured over. Dennis went home to his wife and baby son and for a while the story faded away as attention switched back to the remainder of the Tour de France. There was speculation and rumour on social media but Dennis, usually forthright and vociferous, stayed silent.

Was Dennis about to retire? Was he experiencing some kind of breakdown? With stage wins in all three Grand Tours to his name, alongside five World Championships on the track and road, the Hour Record in 2015 and a host of other accomplishments, Rohan Dennis was one of the finest cyclists Australia had ever produced, and at 29 he surely had several more years to win more? What had gone so wrong?

Gradually a picture emerged of a dysfunctional relationship between a rider and his team. Dennis was known to be a demanding athlete, always pushing for what he felt would help him go faster, and not shy in arguing his case. Throughout the first half of the season Dennis had been unhappy with the equipment being offered to him. He saw other riders with more aerodynamic clothing, equipment and bikes and was frustrated that his own team couldn't offer him the same. They were, like all professional cycling teams, constrained by their sponsorship contracts. Dennis had independently tested some new skinsuit options in the wind tunnel at the Chris Boardman Performance Centre in Worcestershire, and found one he liked. The moment that apparently tipped him over the edge was when he was told during the Tour de France that the team would not allow him to use his preferred skinsuit.

During August and September, after his very public departure from the Tour de France, Dennis stayed at home in Australia and didn't race, talk to journalists or post on social media. His team, snubbed by their star rider, wanted to terminate his contract. Crucially, during this time Dennis spent a lot of time with sports psychologist Dr. David Spindler, whom he credits for his eventual return to racing.

Spindler works with athletes to understand and unlock how their welfare and psychology affects their performance. Through his research and experience he has gained a deep understanding of the pressures on athletes, particularly on cyclists, and the resulting issues that can arise. Cycling is a very traditional sport. Professional road teams have not historically been very good at looking after their riders or trying to understand their psychology. The attitude is: get on your bike and ride. If there is pressure: deal with it. Inevitably there are many casualties along the way. Spindler points to two groups of cyclists that are particularly under pressure − first-year professionals who, barely out of their teens, have only two years to prove themselves to their team, and older riders who have children. Having a baby, Spindler has pointed out, changes everything for a rider. He no longer wants to spend most of the year travelling, and the dangerous aspects of cycling take on more significance. And because teams are so ill-equipped to support their riders through these pressures, the rider stays silent while their stress level rises and rises, culminating in some kind of crisis. This is broadly what happened to Dennis, though talking to Spindler during that crisis helped to save his career.

Underpinning Spindler's work with athletes is his research as a cognitive neuroscientist. When Dennis came to him in the summer of 2019, Spindler was completing a PhD that sought to understand the idea of 'happiness watts'.

When he began his PhD, Spindler wanted to understand how elite athletes make decisions when they are performing above their threshold power. How does the brain function when an athlete is under severe physiological stress? Working with cyclists at the New South Wales Institute, Spindler had observed that some riders made better tactical decisions during races, when riding full tilt, and those riders invariably achieved better results. When he asked the riders why they thought that was, they replied 'happiness watts'. This is the idea that riders who are happy produce more power and make better cognitive decisions. Spindler decided he wanted to test this idea scientifically.

Initially he did a lot of reading about how happiness manifests itself in the brain, then about how military personnel perform when under severe stress in a combat zone. Then he put together experiments to test the cognitive abilities of elite athletes under a range of emotional scenarios. The athlete was asked to cycle at their threshold (that is, at a level of exertion they could only maintain for around an hour) and perform cognitive tasks. Meanwhile Spindler and his team manipulated the athlete's emotions.

The outcome was clear. Happiness watts can be proven. The higher the levels of dopamine and serotonin (the chemicals in the brain which cause happiness) and the lower the level of cortisol (the stress chemical), the more power he or she produces. These chemicals do not change an athlete's physiology. Instead they delay the point where the brain says to the body, "Look, we are exhausted, it's time to stop." In other words, a happy athlete keeps producing their optimal power for longer. A stressed or unhappy athlete ceases their effort sooner.

Spindler also found that cognitive fatigue could undermine performance. If an athlete was mentally tired because he'd been playing computer games all night or spending hours on Twitter, his time to exhaustion would decrease in much the same way as if he was unhappy.

The implications were clear. If coaches and doctors could find ways to make their athletes happier, and well rested mentally, they could improve performance. The athlete would get more out of their body because their brain would delay the point at which it wanted to stop.

Dennis' unhappiness with his team during 2019 had been multi-faceted. The management there had been unable, or unwilling, to find better ways to work with their rider. And the result was a pressure cooker of frustration in Dennis' mind. By the Tour de France he thought that the situation was a threat to his marriage, and that he would become just another divorced sportsman. When his unhappiness got to that point, he cracked and pulled over at the side of the road.

Two months later Dennis arrived in Harrogate for the UCI Road World Championships to defend his time-trial crown. It was, he said, the biggest job interview of his life. Riding for Australia and aboard an unbranded bike of his own choosing, Dennis knew this was the chance to put his troubles behind him. If he performed well he would show the world that his class was undiminished.

Dennis' wife and baby son travelled to Yorkshire to watch him race. They were the last people he saw before he climbed into the car to drive to the start line in Northallerton, and on the way he posted a picture of himself and his son to Instagram, with the words 'what actually matters'. From the first few kilometres, the result never looked in question. Dennis smashed his way around the rolling 54-kilometre course and finished over a minute ahead of the talented young Belgian Remco Evenepoel. As he came across the line he punched the air in customary fashion. And before he did so he tapped a finger against his helmet to indicate that his victory was a mental one. When he rolled to a stop his wife and son were the first to give him a hug.

What can we take from this story? Putting aside elite sport, in whatever field you are working in, the ambition is usually for a high level of performance. You expect a lot of yourself and a lot of your team. It can be easy, then, to slip into ways of working that are actually counter-productive. Piling on the pressure may get things done in the short term but you will be accruing a weight of frustration and conflict that will inevitably surface at some point. After the World Championships, Dennis' team immediately terminated his contract and he signed for Team Ineos, formerly Team Sky. There, he later told a journalist, Dave Brailsford had created a hard-working and positive environment. Team Ineos are renowned for their attention to detail (that is to say, the marginal gains idea). They listened to Dennis' requests on equipment. They may not have been able to accommodate all his requests, but they listened to him and they respected him, and that is what matters.

Does this mean you should throw a colossal tantrum when things start going against you? Of course not. It means that you should stand up for what you believe will support your performance. And, more importantly, it means you should work out what makes you happy. You are much more likely to achieve your ambitions if you approach them from a place of contentment.

And if you are a team leader, there is a lesson here about leadership. Perhaps Rohan Dennis was demanding, but a strong and confident team manager would have not only identified ways to manage his relationship with Dennis, he would have embraced Dennis' rigour. By listening to Dennis and taking his questions seriously, the team manager could have improved his rider's performance and then used the same methods to improve the performance of the whole team. A leader has to think about how to get the best out of his team. In Team KGF we listened to each other and made the effort to take each other's point of view seriously. That was important. If I suggested something, even if it ultimately did not proceed, I could feel sure I would be listened to.

16

Get professional help

Mehdi Kordi is not your average cycling coach. After finishing his degree in Biomedical Sciences at the University of Manchester, Mehdi worked as a researcher at King's College, London, studying the effects of being in space upon the human body. He created a new CPR technique to be used in space, then went on to study the effects of training in the bones and muscles of young military recruits. Between 2011 and 2013 he lived in Cologne, Germany, working at the European Astronaut Centre (part of the European Space Agency) collecting and analysing data from their astronaut selection process.

During this time, Mehdi was also an accomplished athlete. His chosen sport was rowing, and in 2012 he won the Thames Challenge Cup at the prestigious Henley Royal Regatta, before which he flew back from Germany every weekend to train with his club after training by himself during the week. Just as I combined my research and experience in aerodynamics with cycling, Mehdi saw an opportunity to combine his academic achievements with his passion for sport. From astronauts to athletes. However, his first love, rowing, was not open to modern scientific methods. Here is a sport similar to track cycling in its blend of endurance and power, and also culturally – rowing has a long tradition of early-morning training sessions in which the principal method is to get the miles in. In the British rowing establishment this approach has persisted long after other sports, like cycling, have moved on, principally because of the lack of new thinking in its coaching staff. Jürgen Grobler, the head coach of the British squad until 2020, when he retired, was a dominant force in the sport. And phenomenally successful. With such famous athletes as Sir Steve Redgrave and Sir Matthew Pinsent he won so many Olympic gold medals that his methods were beyond question. For the athletes that were not suited to this type of training, this became a frustrating situation. Getting themselves into a position where they might be selected for the Olympic squad was, in itself, a long and tough fight. When they got there, understandably, they were too exhausted or scared to challenge Grobler's methods. He believed in the traditional way of training – lots of miles on the water and on the rowing machine, or the 'erg' as rowers refer to it. Many of the athletes understood the drawbacks of this approach but felt unable to say anything. There was no discussion allowed about alternative ways to train – it was Grobler's way or leave the team. After all, it is hard to argue with someone whose team has won a gold medal at every Olympics between 1972 and 2016.

As a PhD student Mehdi began working at the English Institute of Sport and British Cycling, focusing on the sprint teams. He used his knowledge to challenge current training dogma and introduce his own methodologies to training and performance. His first coaching job was exclusively with the Paralympic sprint tandems. Mehdi introduced a new selection procedure for the British squad, set training plans and coached the riders to much higher levels of performance than they had been achieving before. Both the men's and women's tandem pairs broke world records under Mehdi's supervision. He went on to play an integral role in developing the whole sprint team, designing and conducting new experiments to assess the physiological determinants of maximal power generation for sprint cyclists. This research formed the backbone of the PhD he completed whilst at British Cycling.

In January 2017 Mehdi was standing in track centre when we took on the British Cycling Academy team at the National Championships. We did not know him, and he had not heard of any of us. Despite being a British Cycling coach, our victory – he told us later – brought a smile to his face because it made an event that was usually a boring processional victory for the academy team exciting. He was surprised that a team of amateurs could come out of nowhere and win, yet didn't think much more of it at the time.

Six months later Mehdi saw one of our posts on social media, confirming that we were registered as a UCI trade team and would be going to the World Cups in the 2017–18 season. His interest was piqued, and in September 2017 he got the opportunity to see us in action again, at the Glasgow Grand Prix, where he was coaching the national Paralympic sprint team.

In Glasgow, Mehdi watched us closely. He was intrigued that we were not resting on the laurels of our nationals win and were pushing on to the next level. Saying publicly that we were going to take on the world's best teams at the World Cups was audacious, bold, some would say foolish. It was certainly a different modus operandi compared to the quietly measured approach of British Cycling. We won the qualifying round in Glasgow, then the final with a time of 4:04. As planned, Jonny dropped off after five laps, leaving the three of us to grind out the remaining 12 laps. Mehdi could see what was going on. Jonny had a high anaerobic capacity and we were using him in the most efficient way possible. We seemed to be good on aerodynamics and engineering, but he rightly identified that our changes were untidy. And we were operating almost entirely alone. Unlike most teams, we had minimal support crew. We did not even have anyone to hold us up on the start line, and had to ask other teams for a favour.

After the event Mehdi approached us and we got chatting. He shared his enthusiasm for the idea of creating a track trade team, we talked about bike position and physiology and as we parted we agreed for him to come to Derby velodrome to see us train. For Mehdi the meeting in Derby, a few weeks later, confirmed what he had suspected. We were good at some things (aerodynamics, thinking creatively about the event) but poor at others (training, physiology, change technique). In training we were just repeating the same kind of session over and over again. Sitting in track centre, as a few other riders whizzed around the track, Mehdi talked us through the kind of power numbers that we would have to produce to be competitive internationally. We were astonished and, secretly, I was pretty daunted. But Mehdi saw our potential. He saw in us a lot of enthusiasm and energy and a willingness to learn. We had raw talent that could be refined.

We were a dysfunctional bunch to work with. Inquisitive, independent, over-confident, ambitious. Our personalities were as disparate as our physiologies. Most of the time we got on well, laughing and joking around like any other group of twenty-something athletes, but there were also times when we could not stand the sight of each other. There were some blazing rows. The house could become a very tense place, particularly as important events approached, and often one of us had to go out for a long walk or bike ride to cool off.

It was hard for Mehdi because he was used to working with athletes who were part of a programme. These athletes were accustomed to doing what they were told without protest. We, in comparison, were used to doing everything ourselves, so while we welcomed his knowledge, we wanted to question everything. It must have been as frustrating for him to explain his physiological calculations over and over again as it was for me to explain my aerodynamic calculations. But Mehdi saw the method in our madness; he saw that we wanted a more democratic model, in which the athletes were empowered with knowledge and felt able to question anything. And he endorsed that culture. If he hadn't endorsed it, Mehdi probably would soon have run screaming out of Derby velodrome. Instead, though, he stayed and became instrumental to our success.

Mehdi was integral to the team. Once a week he came down to Derby for a training session and through the rest of the week we were in constant contact by phone or text. It was a constructive relationship because we all acted as peers. There was no hierarchy, no power games or politics. And there was no money involved. We couldn't afford to pay Mehdi and remain immensely grateful that such a talented and resourceful coach agreed to work with a bunch of misfits with attitude, for free.

During 2017 and beyond, this was a working model that we developed further. It's easy to say that knowledge should be shared freely, but the reality is that experts like Mehdi spend their careers building up knowledge in their specialist area. That has a value. When working for British Cycling and more latterly for the KNWU, the Royal Dutch Cycling Union, for whom he coaches their sprint team, Mehdi worked in a traditional salary model – they paid him for his time and expertise. Because we could not pay him, we settled upon an exchange system – Mehdi gave us insight into physiology and training (amongst many other things) and we gave him insight into aerodynamics and engineering, plus a group of enthusiastic guinea pigs on which to try out his newest ideas.

Later, and in our search for help that we increasingly realised we needed, we began to seek out partners for other aspects of our enterprise – nutrition suppliers, tyre manufacturers, clothing manufacturers, engineering and composites companies – and we always began with the same mindset. Let's create a mutual endeavour, find ways to help each other, and where possible keep money out of the equation. That's not to say that you don't have to think about money at all – it's always there in the back of people's minds as a constraint – but the critical thing is to find the right balance so that both parties feel they are getting something out of the deal. At the start of our journey it felt like we were just a group of chancers and did not have much to offer people who were already experts in their field. Yet we soon realised that many companies were very keen to try out their ideas and products on a professional cycling team who were intelligent, engaged and equally keen to be a part of research and design programmes.

When looking for people to work with, their attitude is as important as their expertise. It does not necessarily have to match your own attitude, but it does have to complement it. Outsiders should bring fresh perspectives and sometimes this might be challenging; they should always do so in the spirit of the enterprise you are embarking on together. Coming into a bigger organisation, the outsider can be constructively disruptive because they have no reverence for the way things have always been done, and they have no vested interests. Employees will always consider their long term within the company. A consultant will say it like it is.

Building partnerships based on an equal exchange of ideas and knowledge, rather than a monetary deal, will always engender more collaborative and creative thinking. It has become one of the most exciting aspects of what we do and I would encourage anyone and everyone to do the same.

17

The importance of local knowledge

In Belgium, the cities of Brussels, Ghent and Kortrijk form a rough triangle, with Kortrijk to the west being closest to the French border. The land in the middle of this triangle is part of West Flanders and if you happened to be passing through, it would probably seem pretty unremarkable. It looks rather like southern England – a mix of agricultural land, affluent villages, some light industry and small towns. Turning off the main road, you would quickly find yourself in a maze of tiny lanes, amid rolling hills, woodland and rich fields.

For racing cyclists this is hallowed ground. For this is where the venerated Tour of Flanders plays out. Created in 1913 by a Flemish newspaper, the Tour of Flanders is a one-day classic road race, one of five 'monuments' of the sport – races that are steeped in history and tradition and are held in the same esteem as the Tour de France. The Tour of Flanders is a symbol of its region, an emblem of national identity (for the Flemish have long seen themselves as a nation, quite separate from the other part of Belgium, Wallonia). The race takes place every April and hundreds of thousands of fans line the twisting route to cheer on their heroes, drink the local beer and consume vast quantities of chips with mayonnaise. There are VIP tents for the businessmen, but the best atmosphere is out on the roadside where the yellow and black Flemish flags wave and loyal cycling fans mix with those lucky enough to live near the course.

For the riders the Tour of Flanders is a unique challenge. It is long, over 250 kilometres, and there are 20 'hellingen', short steep climbs that sting the legs and often provide a springboard for attacks. Many of these climbs are cobbled, making it difficult to maintain a good pedalling rhythm, and if wet the cobbles can become so slippery that just staying upright is a challenge. In the second half of the course most of the roads are tiny lanes, constantly twisting and turning through the fields. They are frequently broken and covered in mud from tractor wheels. And even in the towns and villages the roads are populated with what cyclists ironically call 'street furniture' – bollards, speed bumps and raised kerbs, all of which will have you sitting on your bum nursing a broken collar-bone in an instant.

Because of all these challenges, and because the race is so keenly fought, position is crucial. Any rider who wants to be competitive has to stay near the front of the 200-rider peloton. Slip further back and you risk being caught behind a crash, or simply not being able to react to an attack from one of your rivals. Everyone knows this, so everyone is fighting for position, which in itself causes crashes. So the race is incredibly nervous.

Local knowledge is a significant weapon in a rider's armoury. Those who know the roads have an advantage. They know where the road is rough and how to avoid it; they know the fastest line to take through corners and what they will find around that corner; they know which sections are exposed to the wind; they know the places where a neat bunny hop over a kerb could move them up 20 places. These may seem like tiny gains but, as we have seen before, it is the aggregation of small gains that counts. The rider with local knowledge saves himself just a little stress and energy at each of these moments, and over a six-hour race that adds up. In comparison, the rider who doesn't know the roads is always being taken by surprise, slipping back in the fast-moving group of riders, and then having to fight his way back to the front.

Less frenetic, but equally dramatic, a Tour de France mountain stage can also be won or lost on local knowledge. Long Alpine climbs often have changeable gradients, sections exposed to the elements and many hairpin turns. When a rider is on his physical limit, even a relatively minor change in the climb can make a big difference. So any rider serious about getting a good result in the Tour de France goes to ride the major climbs before the race. Reconnaissance missions are a feature of the Tour's build-up. It is equally important to know the descents. Make a mistake on a fast descent and the consequence could be career-ending, possibly even life-ending.

Road cycling is unusual in the variety of landscapes on which it is played out. This is, of course, part of the reason fans and riders love the sport. From one week to the next a rider might be tackling Belgian cobbles, a monstrous mountain climb in France or the rolling roads of Yorkshire. Most sports are not so varied in their arenas. Indeed many sports precisely stipulate the nature of their competitive environments. A football pitch used for international matches must be, according to FIFA, between 100 and 110 metres long, and between 64 and 75 metres wide. The surface must be grass (FIFA list out acceptable types of grass), the markings must be continuous white lines and the corner flagpoles must be at least 1.5 metres high with a non-pointed top. Precise dimensions are also specified for the goals. Championship tennis courts have a similarly prescriptive set of regulations on size, though with an allowance for different types of surface – grass, clay or synthetic. These different surfaces significantly affect the way the game is played, to the extent that some players are known for being specialists in one or the other.

Even when their arenas are so uniform, elite athletes are finely tuned to the subtle characteristics of their environment. They can feel differences that amateurs cannot. And for an elite athlete, their sense of the environment extends well beyond the field of play. Even if one athletics track is much like another, the athletes will want to know what the changing rooms are like, the size of the warm-up track, where the toilets are, how long is the transfer from the hotel, does the hotel have facilities for them to make their own food... all the way back to the airport. The race is the moment that an athlete delivers his or her performance, yet building up to that moment are dozens of environmental factors that can influence the result. Know the environment and we can plan for it. Follow the plan and stress levels are minimised. As we discovered earlier, those athletes with lower cortisol levels perform better. Happiness watts are there to be taken.

Elite athletes and their support crews are control freaks. In an ideal world they would like to control everything that goes on around them. The next best thing is to take control of the factors that most affect the athlete's performance. That is why Team Sky began taking high-quality, hypoallergenic pillows to races. They understood that a rider getting quality sleep was essential during a multi-day stage race, and the varying quality of hotel pillows put that at risk.

During the summer of 2017, between the training sessions and the arguments about washing-up, we spent time researching the World Cup events we were approaching, the first event being in Poland in November. We were national champions but making the leap to the international stage was an altogether different challenge, logistically as well as physically.

The first step in grasping your environment and the conditions around you is to gain an understanding of all the factors that will affect your performance at the place you are competing. One way to do this is to start by visualising the moment of success – a race won, an exam passed, a business launched – and then walk backwards, through the course and along the process to get to that moment. Write down as many features of the build-up as you can think of. The ones that matter will jump out at you. But pay attention to the rest. Are there any gaps in the process, or activities on which you are a bit hazy? Home in on these, and stop and think. Interrogate your knowledge and do your research. It is worth taking the time to do so. These hazy parts may not seem a big deal now, weeks or months away from your objective. But once you're getting close to the competitive environment, they will suddenly become stressful, much more stressful than they need to be.

Once you have a thorough understanding of the process you will be following, you can begin to plan how you are going to ease your way along it. In elite sport, the aim is always to arrive at the competition calm, well rested and focused. In Team KGF we had a plan for every moment of the process, with clear accountabilities divided between the team members. For breakfast, we knew what each rider needed to eat, who was doing the shopping, who was cooking and who pulled the short straw to get the washing-up. The result was that none of us worried about breakfast (cyclists are obsessive about food, not always in good ways) and we all got the fuel we needed. For the National Championships, if we had not made this plan, the result could have been four young men waking up hungry, realising no one had done any food shopping, then having an almighty argument about it while driving around suburban Manchester on a Sunday morning looking for somewhere that served porridge. Not a good start to race day.

As summer turned to autumn in that pivotal year of my life, the prospect of racing internationally grew ever more real. Our World Cup campaign would start in November and run through to January – if the money did not run out first. It was time to turn theory into results.

Part 6

Be ready to change the plan

18

Learn lessons quickly

November 2017, Pruszków, Poland
– UCI World Cup Round 1

For all our efforts to understand the competitive environment for our first World Cup, the reality was disorienting and frustrating. We decided that it would be wise to choose one of the UCI-recommended hotels. It was not what we had hoped for.

Every day there were only two shuttle buses from the hotel to the velodrome, otherwise it was a three-kilometre walk. There were no cooking facilities and no food storage. We improvised and took advantage of the cold Polish winter, storing all perishables out on our windowsills. Within a few hours the hotel management spotted our improvisation and asked us to stop. We had been assured over email that food was included in the price of the rooms, but the hotel's idea of food turned out to be a shrink-wrapped breakfast with cured meats and terrible cheese. No fruit or vegetables. Certainly not enough to fuel a day's riding.

Hungry and frustrated, we travelled to the velodrome, hoping to find more nourishment at the restaurant there. When the shuttle bus had crawled its way through the morning traffic, we made our way to the restaurant, only to find that for riders they were charging €20 per person per meal. We definitely could not afford that. Ellie begged the restaurant staff and explained our situation. They let us share plates, and then fill our Tupperware afterwards. It effectively cut our food costs by 75 per cent.

Our preparation for Poland had gone pretty much to plan. During the summer we had taken part in road races and time trials, keeping the fitness ticking over without putting ourselves under too much stress. For us, the summer was the off-season and an opportunity to build endurance by doing longer events. In August we regrouped at Derby Arena and focused once more on our speed and power, and the discipline of riding as a unit. All through the year we had been tweaking our equipment, testing new bits of kit and adjusting our riding positions. In September and October it was time to bring all that together.

After a four-week block of hard training, we tapered off – what athletes call the period when they rest their bodies before a competition in order to arrive fresh. I was flying. As soon as I got on to the track in Poland I could feel the benefit of all those exhausting sessions on the Derby track and in the gym.

It felt exciting to finally be at a World Cup, with all the UCI banners around the building, the national teams in the track centre and the announcer testing the sound system in Polish and stilted English. Having been used to domestic racing, just the internationality of it was motivating. For so long I had wanted to get to this level, and now we were here, on the start sheet.

We walked around the track centre in awe of everything around us. If any of us thought we would try to play it cool, we utterly failed. Before the racing there were official training sessions. Every team gets some time on the track to get a feel for it, keep the legs ticking over and familiarise yourself with the unique aspect of each track. All the teams before us were riding round at a conservative pace, spinning around in big groups. This was just part of their routine, not a big deal.

When our turn came the excitement was too much. Our plan for the training sessions was to get used to the track and to assess how our legs felt by riding a steady pace. Instead of doing that we wound up the pace until we were doing personal best lap times. I felt so good that my legs hardly hurt, despite the blistering speed. We were trying too hard to show everyone that we had arrived, that there was a new kid on the block. And the opposition did take notice; coaches from the French and Italian teams stood together ignoring their own riders and watching us. Who were these random Brits going so fast?

In qualifying we finished eighth, with a time of 4:01.6, beating established countries like the United States and Belgium, and less than three seconds off the fastest time, set by Italy. Our time was good enough to get us into the rounds, and I knew we could go faster, a lot faster. But in qualifying Tipper had been riding on his limit, screaming 'Hold' at us during the last two laps, so if we were to go under four minutes for the first time, he would have to perform better. Our opponents in the rounds would be Switzerland, who had qualified a second faster than us. I had done my research. Switzerland were not one of the quickest teams. If we put together a decent performance, we should be able to beat them.

We started strongly, too strongly. By the time Jonny peeled off, having done his turn on the front, we were on for a 3:55, our fastest ever time. Charlie did his turn, with me next in line. When you are feeling good you want to be on the front so you can absolutely bury yourself into the effort. Getting to the front becomes an all-consuming desire. You just know that you can take the pace up a notch and show the world just how fast you are. Of course, quite often you can feel this way and then when you hit the front – and lose the benefit of slipstreaming another rider – you are not able to go as fast as you'd hoped.

Charlie swung up the track and slotted back down behind me. I still felt good and focused on maintaining the same pace that Charlie had been riding at – apparently effortlessly. But Tipper was in trouble. I heard someone shout from behind 'Hold!' so I slowed the pace a little. Then a lap later I heard the shout that no one wants to hear in a team pursuit: 'Two!' There were only two of us left – me and Charlie. Tipper had dropped off the back, unable to keep up with us. It was a disaster. With the time taken on the third man, and Tipper riding alone, our official time was going to be horribly slow. We rode the last six laps with me on the front. Charlie and I rode a 3:58 and beat Switzerland but finishing with two men counts for nothing. Many agonising seconds later the gun was fired as Tipper crossed the line.

I was angry, sickened, disappointed. Unable to believe what had just happened. After climbing off our bikes in the track centre we sat on our chairs in silence. When the words began to come they were mostly obscene. Tipper was in tears.

It was a mortifying performance. We had really showed how not to ride a team pursuit. Shown ourselves as the amateurs we were. I hated the idea that the other teams might be laughing at us. The whole situation was crushing. It was frustrating because I knew we could do better. Our ride in qualifying demonstrated that. Yet it all meant nothing if we could not organise ourselves to finish together.

November 2017, Manchester, UK
– UCI World Cup Round 2

On the flight home from Poland, Tipper and Charlie ended up in seats on their own, and Jonny and I were sitting next to each other. This was probably for the best. Tipper was, understandably, still in a very bad place. He felt that he'd let the team down, and that if it wasn't for him we'd have beaten Switzerland and gone into the finals. We tried to comfort him and brush off his apologies, but the truth was that we all felt the same way. Three of us had great form for Poland, one did not, and that cost us dearly.

By the time we boarded the plane my head had begun to come around. Yes, we were all devastated because we could have beaten Switzerland and in the process recorded a really fast time. Perhaps even a 3:55. That meant we were not terrible. We could have been up there with the top teams, but for our one weakness.

The second World Cup in Manchester was one week away. Our budget was running out, so it looked likely that Manchester would be our last international event as a team. We had to learn from Poland, otherwise the same thing would happen and the other teams would definitely laugh at us – it's one thing to make a mistake, but it's another thing not to learn from it. And this time we would be racing on home turf in front of family and friends.

In Poland most of the national teams we had been competing against had a support crew of 10 to 12 people, and the coaches are the dominant figures. In these programmes, for every four riders on the track there are another four back home who did not get picked. And while the World Cups are important, these teams are ultimately focused on one thing – the Olympics. Even if the Games are three years away, the Olympics are what they obsess about. All of which creates a situation in which it is in no one's interests to be honest. If a national team had as disastrous a race as we had in Poland, they would not have examined themselves as rigorously and as honestly as we did. The coaches, not wanting to accept blame, would have glossed over it, taking comfort from there being plenty of time to correct mistakes before the Olympics. And the riders, fearful of losing their spot on the team, would not have accepted blame either. So while there would have been a debrief and some gloomy faces, it's unlikely a national team really would have examined their performance as if their collective careers depended on it.

As we sat on that uncomfortable plane flying back from Poland, Jonny and I agreed that not only did we have to solve a problem like Tipper, we also had to push ourselves to go after further gains. So we found a pen and paper and began writing. On that flight we wrote a list of 43 ways to make the team go faster. The list included simple things like changing to bigger gears, details about our preparation such as increasing Tipper's caffeine levels, how our bikes were set up, and the possibility of Charlie and I riding the event as a two-man unit, with Tipper just hanging on to our back wheels and never coming on to the front. We even considered putting Tipper in a luxury hotel the night before the race so he could sleep well and feel happy.

Importantly, we hit on the idea of organising our strategy with the objective of protecting Tipper. In a line of four riders, the man at the back, man four as we call him, benefits most from the slip-stream effect. If Tipper was our weakest link, we had to shepherd him to the finish. This meant keeping him out of the wind.

Back in Derby we discussed this idea with Mehdi and he hit upon strategic gold. If, after my opening turn on the front, I could drop into third place in the line, ahead of Tipper, then he would not hit the front until the last few laps. Keeping him further back in the line for longer, where the aerodynamic drag reduction is greater in the draft, would reduce his overall workload. It also meant he had less distance to hold on after his half-lap turn, just two laps to the finish. Mentally that was a lot more achievable. It was a novel approach and we termed it the Mehdi Method in honour of its originator. None of us could remember ever seeing any team try it. Orthodoxy was the front rider swings up the track and slots in at the back. For me to slot into third position meant Tipper would have to swing up slightly at precisely the right time, a sort of mini-change. Too early and he would be sitting out in the air, riding harder than he needs to. Too late and I would have nowhere to slot in. The risks were high. Ease back too much and he would have a gap to close down, using up valuable energy. Ease back not enough and our wheels would clip, likely bringing us down.

In Manchester we set about trying out as many of the 43 items on the list as we could during our allotted training sessions. Mentally, that was a tough week. The tension was high, and our usual jokey team dynamic was gone. Nothing negative was said, but then it didn't have to be. We all knew what was going on. This was the downside of being an independent, self-supported team. All four of us had invested a lot in this project and it felt as though that investment was on a knife-edge. If we screwed up in Manchester as we had in Poland then we'd effectively just wasted a year of our lives. What we needed during those two weeks was an outside perspective, someone to bang our heads together and tell us not to worry so much – it's only a bike race. We had Mehdi working with us, but he was doing it as an unpaid side-project and couldn't commit as much time to it as he would have liked. Sometimes the cool detachment of a full-time professional coach or manager has its benefits.

Physically too, I found it a difficult period. I had picked up a bug on the journey back from Poland (likely on that otherwise productive flight) and by the time we arrived in Manchester I was wiped out. The first training session left me feeling totally drained. I told the others how I was feeling and we agreed to focus only on practising the Mehdi Method, at a relatively slow pace. During the whole week I did just one full-effort training session.

In cycling, the longer you are around the sport, the more resilience you build up. It is a hard sport. You lose more than you win (this is true of everyone, even the best in the world). You crash, suffer mechanicals at inopportune moments, get sick from training in the cold and wet... and yet still you carry on because you love the sport. Tipper came up the hard way. He was never on a development programme. His progress was self-funded and self-motivated. He has learnt to use difficult times as a catalyst to bounce back.

Though that week before Manchester was heavy going, I was pleased about the way we had handled the disappointment of Poland. We drilled into the root causes of the problem in Poland and did not shy away from the reality of the situation. It would have been too easy to make excuses and not face up to the real problems. To learn lessons from your mistakes requires a degree of detachment. We left our emotions behind and tried to think clearly, logically. The pressure of time we were under meant we had to go through this process within 24 hours of racing in Poland. The quick turnaround also meant that everything was fresh in our minds. Those 43 items came like a deluge – the flight from Poland to the UK was not a long one. And many of them were not new ideas; it was just that the scenario allowed us to express ideas that, for whatever reason, had never properly surfaced before.

Here was reverse engineering in its most condensed form: we had the goal of performing well in Manchester, our resources were known and could not be changed within the limited time frame, and we had established that a performance gap had to be bridged if we were to accomplish our goals. Therefore we had to take as many lessons as possible from recent experience and apply them to optimise our chances of performing better.

Before the qualifying session at Manchester we agreed to use our new tactic of me dropping back to man three rather than man four, to give Tipper longer at the back. However, when the moment came I swung up on to the velodrome banking, glanced down and saw no gap to drop into. Tipper was still stuck to the wheel in front, so either he had forgotten or was ignoring the plan. Cursing, I adjusted my trajectory and latched on to the end of the line instead. With our plan ripped up we had to ride on instinct. Fortunately, Tipper was having a better day than he did in Poland and was able to stay with us all the way to line.

This is the reality of any competition. You can set strategies as much as you like but in the heat of competition things change very quickly. You have to be able to adapt to what is going, rather than blindly following a plan that no longer makes sense. In our team pursuit rides, if Charlie feels good he will kick through on to the front and put us all into a world of pain just to stay on his wheel. Which in turn means that you have to accept your own turn on the front is going to be slower and harder because you have used up energy accelerating to follow Charlie. If Tipper forgets the plan and doesn't let me into the line ahead of him, our planned sequence has to change. With experience, you can race on instinct. And when you race on instinct as a team it is particularly rewarding. Regardless of the result, our ability to adjust our plan mid-race was one of the most encouraging things about that qualifying ride in Manchester.

We qualified fifth fastest with 4:00.4 and progressed to a race against Belgium in the rounds. On the start line all of us took a moment to remind Tipper that he had to let me into position three. This time, he heard us and it worked. Our execution was flawless and we rode to a 3:58.134, beating the Belgians by just over a second, and booked a bronze medal ride-off against the European champions, France.

The roar of the crowd as our names were announced before that bronze medal race was electrifying. Of course, many people there understood our story – that less than 12 months before we had taken a surprise victory in the National Championships on this same track. And we all had friends and family in the grandstands, cheering us on. For the first time I had a sense that our story was becoming bigger than just us, and that cycling fans were following our performances. Ten months earlier we had been the disruptors, surprising the establishment. Now our role was slightly different. Our narrative was that of the classic underdog. The establishment wanted to snuff out our flame; the crowd wanted to give it oxygen.

Perhaps the atmosphere got to us because we started fast and with two laps to go we were marginally ahead. But the Frenchmen on the opposite side of the track were not about to be embarrassed by four young upstarts. They dug deep and maintained their pace just at the moment that I began to explode. Atmosphere and exciting underdog narratives will never quite trump pure physiology. In the last lap I could barely hold on to Charlie's wheel. The pain of doing so was horrible. The finish could not come quickly enough. When we crossed the line we were a second behind our opponents.

I was disappointed but it was a very different feeling to that I had experienced in Poland. Fourth place seemed respectable and, looked at objectively, we had come a long way in two weeks. We had proven our potential and that was a kind of redemption. After Manchester the other teams treated us with more respect too. Most of them seemed to quite like having this crazy bunch of British amateurs around. We certainly brought more fun and atmosphere to the event than our compatriots...

Our next World Cup was to be in Minsk, Belarus in January. Ever since I had started planning the World Cup campaign I had been thinking that Minsk would be our best opportunity to perform to our fullest potential. This was part logic, part hunch. I knew it would take us a little while to find our feet at that level. It was unrealistic to expect that we would simply turn up in Poland and destroy the opposition. By January, however, I thought we would have settled in and picked up a few lessons along the way. Belarus was going to be the big one. We had a new goal. We were going to smash it. We were going to win.

19

When things go wrong

That evening as we drove back from Manchester to Derby, the mood was quiet and reflective. None of the usual banter and joking. We were all exhausted, not so much from the racing, but from the mental stress of the last two weeks.

I was quietly satisfied with the way things had gone. Naturally we wanted to do better than fourth, but our closeness to winning bronze, and the way we had turned around our performance since Poland, reassured us that we were on the right trajectory. The next World Cup, in Minsk, was scheduled for mid-January, so we had 10 weeks to reassess and build further. During December we had two races scheduled: the Troféu Anadia in Portugal, which Charlie and I rode for Individual Pursuit World Championship qualification points, and the UCI Track Cycling Challenge, a race meeting in Grenchen, Switzerland, close to the UCI headquarters. This was a prestigious event and we wanted to see how much faster we could take our times there. It would also be a good opportunity to test new ideas or equipment in a race setting. Our original team budget had almost run out so, buoyed by our success in Manchester, we agreed to all put some more money in ourselves. When you collectively have close to £100,000 of student loans debt, another £2,000 each does not make much of a difference.

Three days after we came back from Manchester we were at Derby Arena for a training session. Our focus that day was on starting efforts. In a team pursuit the four riders line up across the track at the start line. To enable us to clip into our pedals, four helpers stand behind us and hold us up by holding on to the rails under our saddles. The pedals we use are similar to ski bindings; a plastic cleat containing a metal spring on the sole of our shoes clicks in, locking the shoe to the pedal. The only way for that shoe to detach from the pedal is for the rider to twist his heel outwards. That's the theory anyway.

When the starting electronic beeps sound, all four riders have to get up to full speed as quickly as possible. This means a huge initial effort to get the gear turning and the bike moving. Turning the cranks from a dead stop, on a gear designed for riding at 65 kilometres per hour, is very similar to weightlifting. It's all about strength and technique. Our times for the first 200 metres in Manchester were respectable, but not on a par with Great Britain, who won the gold medal, so there was definitely room for improvement.

It was during one of these intense starting efforts that Jonny's foot unclipped from the pedal. He had a little wobble and corrected it by applying a sideways force on his pedal, which caused it to twist out. He was travelling fast through turn two, where typically you produce your peak power and torque, and the next thing he knew he was flying over the handlebars and down the track. In such moments time seems to slow down. Afterwards Jonny said he could see the black line on the track coming towards him, and he simply thought, *Oh shit!*

He landed heavily on his left shoulder and once the world had stopped tumbling, he sat, still and dazed, on the track. Straight away he knew the consequences. It was his first big crash and his first broken collarbone. Spend some time with a group of elite cyclists and you'll soon realise how common collarbone breaks are. A scar across a shoulder blade is almost a badge of honour. Jonny sat on the track holding his arm and staring at the bone sticking out underneath his skinsuit.

Fuck it, I've ruined it for everyone, was one of his first thoughts. And he verbalised this for everyone in the track to hear, and probably a few out in the car park too. The next was: get me off the track – the other guys can't train with me sitting here. The velodrome staff carried Jonny off the track and gave him some painkillers while they waited for paramedics to arrive.

In hospital, waiting on his own in a room, still wearing only his ripped skinsuit, the emotion hit him. It was only 63 days until Minsk, the biggest race of his career as an athlete. Starting with only three riders isn't allowed, and there was no one else who could step in. Either he made it back, or our project was over. He cried and cried, and when the doctors came to see him he told them he was a professional athlete and that he was in training for the Commonwealth Games. This was sort of true...

The team at the Royal Derby were amazing. They rescued our own team and the rest of our season by working to mend Jonny quickly and effectively. The crash happened on Wednesday afternoon and by Friday afternoon his surgery was complete and he was in recovery. They could have done it sooner, but because he was a professional athlete they ordered the best pins and screws they could get hold of.

There was never any question of Jonny letting the crash defeat him. He is a resilient person. I knew that because of everything he had been through, and because of how much we needed him, he would fight his way back to fitness as soon as he could. Because he was often loud and exuberant at the track, other teams perceived Jonny as a bit of a joker. But I understood that his self-appointed role of chief morale officer was really only a character he played to mask how he was really feeling. Indeed it had started as a way to help the team. Charlie and Jonny were close friends and Jonny knew that Charlie often got very nervous before races. He also knew that if he could make Charlie laugh during those tense minutes before a race, it would break the nerves, and Charlie would relax a little. So Jonny clowned around in track centre and made Charlie laugh, giving those around us the idea that was how Jonny always behaved. Jonny's attitude to racing may have seemed casual but because of his struggles with depression, it was anything but. When it came to preparing for races, of the four of us he was the most serious.

20

What is a team?

Looking at the situation objectively, with Christmas approaching, we agreed that we needed to plan for the worst. If Jonny was not fit for the UCI Track Cycling Challenge in December, we had to find a replacement. The obvious candidate was Harry Tanfield. Harry had just completed a successful road season, riding for a British team that was beginning to venture to races in mainland Europe, and was now stuck at home in Yorkshire, doing his winter training and perhaps a little bored. We sensed that Harry was also a little jealous of this exciting project his younger brother was engaged in. Physically, Harry was a natural fit. His anaerobic capacity was similar to his brother, he was used to holding an aero position, and he knew how to endure the pain of a short fierce effort. He had just finished second at the National Time Trial Championships, just behind Geraint Thomas and ahead of Alex Dowsett. Having not raced much on the track, though, his starting technique was not great. However, we all agreed that could be sorted out fairly quickly.

Jonny was making good progress as the UCI Track Cycling Challenge in Grenchen approached, and showed in training that he was nearly back to his best, so we travelled to Switzerland as a team of five. Harry understood that he was our insurance option, should Jonny encounter any problems in the warm-up sessions. But Jonny went well in training and proved himself capable of doing his five-lap turn. So in the qualifying race we lined up with the usual personnel – me, Jonny, Tipper and Charlie.

While each of us were focused on our role in the race, we were also very conscious of Jonny's psychological battle to overcome his fear of crashing again. Usually he gets excited in the run-up to a race because he relishes opportunities to show what he is capable of, and because he feeds off the atmosphere inside a velodrome on race day. But this time it was different. He was afraid. His shoulder was heavily strapped up and was painful – and that pain was a constant reminder of what had happened. Those moments on the start line, as the crowd fell silent and the digital clock ticked down before us, were almost unbearable. Every cyclist experiences that fear after a big accident and the only way to beat it is to get back on your bike and face it.

To reduce the force exerted on his shoulder, Jonny chose to start from a sitting down position. Usually he would bring his bottom a few centimetres off the saddle. Ten seconds to go. Then those electronic beeps that are like a permanent sonic imprint in the minds of track cyclists. Five, four, three, two, one.

One pedal stroke, two pedal strokes. Heave that gear around, pull so hard on the handlebars you would think they might snap, breathe or snort or grunt – whatever works for you. The start of a pursuit race is all about getting from a dead start up to full speed as quickly as possible. Out of the saddle we went sprinting into the first bend, eight disc wheels winding up the volume of their familiar whomp-whomp noise... we were away cleanly. Jonny was safely ensconced behind me in the line. After that it was just a matter of sticking to the game plan. Everyone in the team seemed to be riding well and we qualified fastest by five seconds. We were set up to meet 100% ME in the final the next day, the first time we had raced them since the National Championships in January.

Using Airbnb for accommodation, instead of the expensive hotels that the UCI recommend, was one of the ways in which we saved money that season. It was a lottery, and in Grenchen we won big. Our house was beautifully furnished, had a 60-inch television and a Jacuzzi. The kind of house the four of us could only dream about owning. The only negative was that there were not enough full-size beds. Jonny ended up sleeping on a pink Cinderella-themed bunk bed, which he said was actually very comfortable, as long as he didn't try to straighten his legs.

That evening, back at the house, Jonny took me aside and asked me what I thought about riding Harry in the final instead of Tipper. I could tell Jonny was conflicted about suggesting it because Tipper was a friend, but I admired him for having the courage to bring up what we'd all been thinking since Manchester – that Tipper simply wasn't physiologically as suited to the event as others in the team. He was training well enough but there were limits to what he would be able to achieve, and with Harry in the team we had more options. It was clear that we would ride faster with Harry than with Tipper. Jonny and I went to find the Tanfields and talked the idea over with them. They agreed, though I could read on their faces how uncomfortable the situation made them feel. I'll tell him, said Jonny – it was my idea.

Secretly I was relieved that Jonny took the responsibility for telling Tipper. I hate conflict and the prospect of confronting Tipper with this news filled me with dread. In this respect, Jonny was far more courageous than me. I felt terrible. Tipper had been part of this project from the start. Without him we would not have made it this far, and beyond racing, I considered him a friend. I wanted to remain logical and scientific about this decision yet underneath I felt we were betraying him.

At dinner, Jonny brought the subject up. It wasn't nice, but we tried to cover off all the aspects of the decision – the positives and the negatives; what Tipper would gain from it, what Harry would gain from it and what the team would gain from it. On the surface the conversation was rational but there was an undercurrent of deep emotion running through it. Tipper said very little, listening carefully to the points we were stumbling through. When he realised that he would not be riding in the final, Tipper was so shocked and dismayed that he could not react. I felt for the guy. He had come so far with us, and coming on top of the disappointment of Poland, this must have been a huge blow to him.

It raised an interesting philosophical question about what our team was (not that I thought about it in such terms until much later). Was our team the original quartet? Or was our team something bigger and looser, with room for riders to come and go? In that house in Switzerland, just before Christmas 2017, we made a choice that was to shape all our futures. We decided that the team could go beyond the four of us, that sometimes the interests of the team would be put before the interests of individuals. And we were implicitly stating our ambition; we wanted to win and that imperative came before everything else.

Of course, we were only doing what every other team was doing when they selected riders for races. The difference for us was that we had come from nowhere as a quartet, with minimal outside help. Reverse engineering our approach had made that quartet as fast as it could possibly be, given our resources. Now an opportunity to expand that resource had come about. Harry had come into the team as an option to replace Jonny after his crash, but in the event he became an option to replace Tipper. Our resource had expanded, we assessed this new level of resource against the demands of a situation, and selected a team that we thought had the best chance of winning. Reverse engineering is not a fixed process. It allows us to flex and adapt to changing circumstances, whilst always adhering to its principles.

There was a strange and tense atmosphere between the five of us as the final approached. Everyone went through their usual process, but communication was minimal. Tipper was there, helping us where he could. I was sure, from the look on his face, that he didn't really know what to do with himself, and just wanted the whole thing to be over.

For the four of us who lined up for that final against 100% ME, the decision about Tipper gave the race an added emotional dimension. We wanted to prove that the decision had been the right one, and that knowledge put a little extra fire in our bellies. 100% ME did not know what had hit them. We caught and passed them after three kilometres.

When we got home we dispersed to our families for the Christmas break. The trip to Switzerland had proven to be unexpectedly stressful and I was thankful for some time away from the intense bubble of the team.

For a rider in the middle of a race schedule, a little indulgence is allowed on Christmas Day, but only on Christmas Day. During the rest of the period I maintained my training regime, tried to sleep well and not eat too many mince pies. When we returned to Derby in the new year, there were just two weeks until we travelled to Minsk.

* * *

Cycling teams do not have many assets, but they do have a lot of bikes. That's a given. And when a professional level road bike can cost around £10,000, the value of what is in your garage can spiral frighteningly. This is a fact not lost on thieves. We were aware that four Lycra-clad young men living in a small house was probably something of an oddity amongst our neighbours. Soon we understood that Derby's criminal element had noticed us too. Returning from the velodrome two days before we were due to fly to Minsk, we got a nasty surprise. Having just finished our last training session on the track, we had driven home with our track bikes, ready to pack them up the next day. We were in two cars, Jonny and Charlie in the first, me and Tipper in the second. At the house, for no obvious reason, Charlie parked across the front of the drive. Had he pulled into the drive his car would have triggered the automatic outside light, perhaps scaring the thieves off, or at least illuminating what was going on...

The last of the four of us to head into the house, Tipper saw a figure in the darkness, climbing over our back fence, hauling a bike away into the darkness. One of the thieves was hauling bikes and frames and wheels out of our garage, passing them to the next man, who was hurling them over a wall into our neighbour's garden. Beyond that garden was a public park, which was clearly their getaway route. Tipper shouted, 'Run! We've been broken into!'

I was already inside the house in my socks, so I turned and ran blindly around the front of the house and towards the park, but the two figures were too quick. They dropped the frames they had been holding and scaled the wall with the agility of men who had done this many times before. They seemed fairly professional. Or perhaps they were setting up their own UCI track team and, having reverse engineered the problem of having no bikes, had opted to steal ours. Whoever they were, they got away with some very expensive road bikes. We did, thankfully, still have our track bikes in the cars. Minsk was still on.

21

The process pays off

January 2018, Minsk, Belarus – UCI World Cup Round 5

Arriving in Minsk, which was covered in a thick blanket of snow, I felt confident that we had done as much as we could to put us in with a chance of victory. Since Grenchen we had continued to tweak our aerodynamics, our training, our clothing – all the usual levers. But perhaps the most promising thing was that we now had five riders on good form. The shock of what happened in Grenchen had prompted Tipper to take action. He began to train harder, to eat and rest properly, and in only three weeks we could begin to see an improvement. There was, however, still a great deal of rancour about his ejection from the starting line-up. That would take a lot longer to resolve.

We again risked the UCI hotel, mostly because the Belarusian Airbnb selection was terrible and oddly expensive. The hotel had a tinge of green everywhere: green carpets, green walls, green sheets, green bathrooms. Really weird. The only place where there wasn't any green was on the plates at dinner. The hotel food was so poor that we resorted to the local supermarket, buying frozen vegetables which we kept outside in the snow (it was minus 14 degrees and we had no fridge or freezer). We then cooked them in hot water out of the coffee machine. Harry can be thanked for his ingenuity there.

The 20-minute walk to and from the track was cathartic. Throughout the weekend the weather was clear and cold. Walking to the track separated us from everyone else who sat in the shuttle buses. They timed the buses to allow athletes to get to the training sessions 30 minutes before the session began, which was fine if you had a full support team already at the velodrome to get your bike and equipment ready. We didn't have any support team so we just had to suck it up and walk. I found it a good time to just talk – walking always is.

On our first day at the velodrome the focus was not on the team but on Charlie, who was due to ride the individual pursuit. Charlie is a talented bike rider, but before we got together as a team his biggest challenge at the time was confidence. Being dropped by British Cycling, for no clear reason, really knocked him. Understandably, when you are 16 you do not question the national team's coaches. For them to drop him from the programme seemed like a pronouncement on his limited future as a cyclist, despite the fact that at the National Championships in January he'd ridden the individual pursuit and recorded an incredible 4:22, with scant preparation. Once he moved to Derby, joined us, focused on the track, brought in new bikes and got himself in a better position, his personal best came down to 4:14, but we knew he was capable of more.

In qualifying he said he felt blocked, that his legs were heavy. Nevertheless he clocked 4:15, the fastest time, setting up a final against Ivo Oliveira of Portugal. The way his legs felt in qualifying worried him as he sat waiting for the final, later that day. He began questioning himself. Carefully, those of us who knew him best talked to him, and stirred up the self-belief he had been building all through the previous year. Settling himself on his bike on the start line, Charlie told himself just to relax and enjoy it.

Charlie may have doubted himself but we never did. He was just in a different class to Oliveira. From the first lap he was ahead, and the result was never in doubt. He was going so fast that halfway through the race I wondered whether he might catch his opponent. It didn't happen, but then catching your opponent is never really the objective for a pursuit racer. Winning comes first, a fast time comes second. Charlie won, and his time sent a shock wave through the track cycling world. A time of 4:12, a new stadium record and only 1.7 seconds slower than the world record set by Jack Bobridge back in 2011. It was also the second fastest time ever by a Briton, faster than Bradley Wiggins' Olympic-winning ride by three seconds. The only faster time was recorded by Chris Boardman using the now-illegal 'superman' position, in which a rider has his arms stretched out over the front of the bike.

This was a coming-of-age performance by Charlie, who at only 21 still had plenty of time to get even faster. We could sense a proverbial eyebrow being raised among the Great Britain coaches. Having helped Charlie on his path towards this moment, I experienced a new kind of emotion as I watched him fly to victory. It made me so happy to see him step up to become the rider we all knew he could be, and that happiness was bound up with pride in my own role. This was, I realised, the pride of a coach whose athlete achieves his goals. It felt very different to the sort of pride I'd felt when riding with the three others in the team pursuit. It was simpler because I wasn't analysing my own performance on the track, and there was a paternal aspect to it – even though I'm only five years older than Charlie. Most of all, it felt good to help someone else reach his goals without there being anything in it for me.

The team pursuit would follow the standard structure for World Cups: qualifying, rounds then finals. In the qualifying race we decided to rest Tipper. Jonny, Charlie, Harry and I recorded 3:57.202. Then in the rounds we swapped Tipper in for Charlie. This seemed to me a good use of our resources. It meant Tipper could go really deep in the rounds because he didn't need to save anything for the final, and Charlie would be fresh for the final, assuming we got there. It was, of course, hard on Tipper. He accepted it with good grace when the plan was discussed in the hotel, though we could all tell his emotions were running hot under the surface.

Channelling all that anger, Tipper put in a brilliant ride. He wanted to prove to himself that he was making a contribution to the team, and when he came through to the front he put in four laps in just over 56 seconds, a phenomenal pace that was only just off world-record splits. That turn of his secured victory over Switzerland, nearly catching them in the process and recording a 3:57.128. It was a joyful moment for Tipper, as it was the Swiss who caught him on the line in that lonely pursuit back in Poland where it all went wrong.

But his happiness did not last very long. In the track centre afterwards Tipper couldn't talk to any of us. He walked away, tears in his eyes, as he realised he wasn't going to be part of a final that we were well capable of winning. He had been working for a year to get to this point and now he was not going to ride in the final, he wasn't going to be on the podium and he wasn't going to get a medal.

It was evening now. Outside it was dark and snowy, but inside the lights were blazing, the music blaring from speakers hanging high above us, and the grandstands were full for this final evening session of a weekend of racing. In the final, we were to face a Russian team, Lokosphinx. While it was registered as a trade team, Lokosphinx was virtually their national team. One of the bikes stolen in the burglary a few days earlier had been the road bike I usually used to warm up on before track races. Instead I used Tipper's time-trial bike, which was not ideal because the positions on all our bikes are so finely calibrated to each rider. Nevertheless it did the job and I was grateful to have that option.

On the start line, as I settled myself on my bike, I felt curiously calm. Mentally I was in that flow state, entirely focused on what I had to do over the next four minutes, and not concerned with anything else. Beside me was Jonny, then on the outside of the track were Charlie and... Harry?

Where was Harry?

Harry had promised his family, who were back home in North Yorkshire, that he would ensure the final was live-streamed for them to watch. I was in the start gate and there is a regulation that says once the lead rider is on his bike, the 45-second countdown begins. The clock was ticking down... 40 seconds... 35 seconds... where the hell was Harry?

Frantically we looked around for him. Was he having some last-minute problem with his clothing? If he missed the start we would automatically default and lose the race.

Twenty seconds... I spotted him at the bottom of the ramp which brings riders up to the track. He was trying to explain to two bemused riders from the Chinese Taipei team how to film us and broadcast it on Facebook with his phone. I screamed at him to get moving. He jogged up the ramp as best he could in cycling shoes, looking a little sheepish, hopped on to his bike and clipped his feet into the pedal with 10 seconds to go. It was all so unnecessary, but it was so like Harry.

We got away from the start cleanly but not as fast as we were capable of. Lokosphinx were in the lead by 0.2 seconds as I swung off to let Jonny come through. Here was our secret weapon. Jonny's unique role, and the way his physiology is so suited to it, is the foundation of our team. He judged it just right, not putting the rest of us in trouble, but accelerating just enough so that by the time he had put in his five-lap turn on the front, we were comfortably ahead of the Russians.

Jonny swung up the track and left the three of us to push on to the finish. Now came the pressure – to maintain the pace, to stay together as a unit. Everything except the wheel in front is a blur. Thoughts are scrambled, you race on instinct, trusting the hours and hours of practice already behind us. There were scrappy moments – a ragged change, my wheel nearly touching the one in front – and by the final kilometre I was hurting deeply, just trying to somehow wring every last bit of power out of my body to stay with the Tanfield brothers.

With one lap to go I glanced at Ellie, who was crouched just beyond the finish line holding an iPad that showed our time gap to the opposition. We were 1.5 seconds up, a comfortable gap providing nothing went wrong. Round the final bend, using the natural kick of the track as the banking flattens out, the three of us broke formation and spread across the track for the final few metres. The finishing pistol fired. We had finished in 3:56, more than two seconds ahead of Lokosphinx, and a new track record. It also would have been good enough to win the 2013 World Championships which were held in Minsk.

I was ecstatic. We had done it. We had won a World Cup. A year earlier we were just a bunch of lads from Derby taking an unlikely tilt at winning a National Championship medal. Now we were a successful international track team. Sitting on our bikes on the rollers, slowly turning the pedals round in a pretence of following our warm-down routine, we excitedly chattered about the race. Ellie plonked a white cowboy hat on to Jonny's head. A bottle of Cava (the closest we ever got to champagne at most races) was passed around as our phones started pinging with messages of congratulations. A few minutes later the poor UCI officials tried to start herding us towards the podium as we continued chatting away, drinking Cava and exchanging handshakes with other teams. Meanwhile Harry was filming everything for Facebook on his phone, which he had rescued from the Chinese Taipei team.

Going into that final I knew we had a good chance of winning. Despite the drama of Jonny's injury and the difficult emotions around swapping Tipper for Harry, in Belarus, on the day, everything went right. I was confident that we could win and do so with a quick time. So when we crossed the line and coasted around the track I was not punching the air with the same kind of ferocity that Rohan Dennis did at his World Championship win. My feeling was a deeper sort of satisfaction, mixed with relief. This was not redemption, nor was it revenge. This was the contentment from seeing a plan come together. Underneath my optimism and confidence, there is always some nagging doubt. I do not show it to many people, only those really close to me, and I'm pretty good at managing it. But it is always there lurking under the surface. They are the doubts that drive you to work harder, to think smarter, to dig out those little nuggets of performance that others aren't even thinking about. Those doubts made winning in Belarus taste even sweeter.

With all the official duties done, there was nothing left but to pack up our kit bags, pull on our heavy winter coats and bobble hats and brave the icy temperatures outside. That final walk back to the hotel through the dark and freezing streets of Minsk was very special. We shared the sense of a job well done. Looking back now, that moment feels like a turning point in my life. After that anything seemed possible.

Winning a gold medal has some unexpected benefits. The day after the race Jonny set out from our hotel to walk the short distance to the velodrome, to pack up his bike and various bits of kit that were still in the track centre. He came to a wide, multi-lane carriageway, the kind of road that looked like it should have been really busy with traffic, but was not. He looked right and left, saw nothing coming, and crossed the road. Then out of nowhere an unmarked police car screeched to a halt behind him. Two policemen jumped out, grabbed him and threw him to the ground. Then they picked him up and bundled him into the back of the car, all the time whilst screaming at him in Belarussian (not Jonny's strongest language). The car pulled away with Jonny sitting in between the two policemen. He said his first thought was, I need to call Ellie and his second was, what the hell is she going to do?

Visions of Belarussian prison loomed in his mind. But suddenly Jonny had a stroke of genius; he reached into his bag and pulled out his gold medal. "I'm a cyclist," he said. "I've just won this." That changed everything. The policemen switched to English and relaxed. When they arrived at the police station they asked Jonny to fill in a few forms then told him he was free to go.

Part 7
Stay radical

22

After reverse engineering

Reverse engineering is a process. Like all processes it has an end point. You will achieve your goal, and you will have learnt a great deal along the way. So what comes next? If you are the sort of person who has thrown your heart and soul into this project, it is safe to assume you are the kind of person who is still ambitious. There are always new goals to pursue.

If you choose to tackle something entirely new, perhaps in a different field to your first reverse engineering project, then you will apply the whole reverse engineering process over again. And though any new project may be daunting, you should feel reassured that the process works and you have experience with it. A few years ago there was some talk in the media about whether Sir Dave Brailsford, the leader behind British Cycling and Team Sky's phenomenal success since 2008, could manage the England football team. It never happened, partly because Brailsford loves cycling too much, and partly because the football authorities are too entrenched in traditional thinking. But it is a fascinating proposition. Would Brailsford have been able to turn around England's fortunes using reverse engineering despite having no experience in the game? I think he would. Any knowledge can be learnt. Given enough time, applying the theory of reverse engineering as he did at British Cycling then Team Sky, Brailsford could have changed English football for the better. The question is not whether the process works but whether he would have had the energy to take on such a monumental project.

Since that momentous season of track racing in the winter of 2017–18 I have had the opportunity to work with other cycling teams. Naturally, reverse engineering was the process I brought with me to help them. And if I were ever to go to work in another sport, reverse engineering would be the template I would take with me. Set a goal, take it apart, assess your resources, develop your tools, set the plan in motion and deliver the performance. It's applicable anywhere.

What if you choose to stay in the same team and the same competitive environment? Having achieved your goals the first time around, where do you go next?

From reverse engineering we move into continuous improvement. This is essentially how Team KGF evolved in the months and years following our success in Minsk. The focus was not on making a big jump in performance based on a target end point, but pursuing continuous small improvements to keep us close to the top of our sport.

In the business world, continuous improvement began life as a management approach made famous by the author Masaaki Imai.

His book, entitled *Kaizen*, outlined how Japanese corporations had become so phenomenally successful during the second half of the twentieth century. Kaizen is an amalgamation of Kai, meaning 'change', and Zen, meaning 'for good'. The book was hugely successful itself and the term became adopted into the lexicon of Western management studies. Kaizen is based on teamwork, discipline, organisation, standardisation and, above all, on creating quality circles. These are not dissimilar to the scientific method we discussed earlier in the book – the business acknowledges a problem, employees are empowered to suggest ideas and hypotheses to solve that problem, action is taken to test the hypothesis, and lessons are learnt and recorded.

Now, all major corporations understand that continuous improvement must play a role in their ongoing strategy. There may be moments of stasis, perhaps brought on by complacency, but falling behind the competition will soon wake the leaders up. At successful companies continuous improvement has become part of the day job. And in recent years, organisational psychologists and leaders have begun to recognise the concept of psychological safety.

The term has become well known because of the work of Harvard Business School Professor Amy Edmondson, who published an influential paper on the subject in 1999. More recently Google undertook an extensive two-year study of its teams, seeking to understand why some teams performed better than others. The result overwhelmingly backed up Edmondson's research. Google found that in its high-performing teams the team members felt psychologically safe. That meant they felt confident that mistakes would not be punished.

Giving employees the freedom to make mistakes creates an environment of risk-taking and creativity.

Edmondson looked at hospitals, correlating their clinical outcome rates with their attitude towards failure. She found those hospitals who identified failure were also the most successful for patients. Conversely, those hospitals who did not want to talk about failure, who brushed it under the carpet, were the least successful. Organisations like Google, who create an atmosphere of psychological safety, she called fearless organisations (which is also the title of her book). Fearless not in the sense of being brave, but literally fear-less, without fear in its culture.

We live in a knowledge economy. This is as true in cycle racing as it is in software development. When people come to work they should feel empowered to contribute their ideas and feedback without fear of being dismissed or punished. Whatever journey your team is on, it is a reasonable assumption that something will go wrong. The important thing is to just accept that and move on.

23

Working with others

After the realisation of our ambitions in Minsk, my focus began to shift from engineering solutions for myself to engineering solutions for others. I was still racing but I relished the new challenge of working with others to help them achieve their objectives.

During January 2018 I was contacted by a top-flight women's road team, Canyon//SRAM Racing. Their manager Ronny Lauke told me that he was concerned about the team's recent performances in team time trials. In 2015 his team had won the team time trial World Championships in Richmond, USA. The following year they slipped to second and in 2017, in Norway, the team had only managed fourth place. They seemed to be on a worrying downward trajectory and he needed help to change direction. Lauke had heard about Team KGF's approach to the team pursuit and conjectured that many of our principles could help his team. He was right; a team time trial is essentially a team pursuit ridden on the road, with six riders, over a distance of roughly 40 kilometres. The world championship event had only been introduced in 2012 and because it always had live television coverage and six rainbow jerseys were up for grabs, it was very important to the team. There was also a sense of pride at work – for a team manager to see his team slowly slipping behind his rivals must have been painful. He wanted to come back strongly at the 2018 World Championships in Austria.

When we first spoke I was about to fly out to Minsk, and did not have the headspace to give the project my full attention. Ronny and I kept talking and agreed that in late spring I would be able to spend some quality time with the team. However, Ronny asked, could I find a way to come to some velodrome aerodynamic testing in Germany in March?

I looked at my diary. There were five days between the end of the Track World Championships in the Netherlands and a training camp in Portugal. I could make it work... just. I flew home from the Netherlands to Birmingham Airport, went home to pack some fresh clothes, and nine hours later was back at the same airport. I flew to Germany, spent three long days with the team at the velodrome at Frankfurt Oder, then flew home, repacked again, and flew out to Portugal. This was not exactly the restful life that most elite athletes are supposed to live.

It was the first of many times that I had to make a choice between developing my career as an athlete and developing my career as a performance engineer. The athlete in me wanted to rest. The engineer in me saw how promising this opportunity was, and what an interesting challenge too.

One of the first things I did with Canyon//SRAM Racing was to spend some time riding on an airfield in Germany, trying out different strategies, practising riding in the line. A team of road racers might only ride three or four team time trials a year, so just spending time on the time-trial bikes, building a consistent level of confidence across all the women, was critical. The team's equipment sponsors were supportive, providing new kit when asked, even if they were rather taken aback at the level of scientific knowledge now being discussed. At times it was challenging to work with equipment partners that I had no pre-existing relationship with. The representative of one sponsor disagreed vociferously with something I had asked for, and then looked a bit sheepish when I explained the mathematics behind my request. It helped a great deal that Ronny always backed me up and explained to his partners that when it came to preparing for the team time trial, I was in charge. This level of support and belief was incredible for me. I had the event in my hands. It was pressured and rewarding, and I seized that opportunity.

In September we travelled to Innsbruck, Austria a week before the race. Every day the team went out on their time-trial bikes and rode the course, sometimes several times in a day. In our first sessions I rode with Ronny in the team car, but soon realised that it was too hard to get a real sense of how the women were riding from there. I switched to my own bike and rode with them, hovering just off the back or to one side of the line, watching the squad closely, filming everything with my onboard GoPro camera, as was every other rider in the team. From that position I was able to spot many of the small mistakes that were happening. It was the same philosophy as being in a team pursuit squad with Team KGF; only by being more or less inside the team could I see what needed improvement.

We documented and analysed every move. In the evenings, at the team hotel, we had a half-hour meeting to discuss what we had done that day. There were some tense moments. Some of the team were reluctant to open up, and some did not react well to constructive criticism. To try to get past the awkward silences, I suggested we go round the room and everyone would offer up a positive and a negative thing that had happened during the day. I encouraged the riders to be honest and if necessary they should point out a mistake made by a team-mate. After all, we agreed, we all want to get faster and we are all grown-up enough to take criticism on the chin. Again, I was simply following the way I had worked with Tipper, Jonny and Charlie. When we were living together this sort of team meeting happened naturally. With Canyon//SRAM Racing it had to be organised more deliberately, but the effect was the same.

The day of the race was cool and overcast. There had been some rain overnight but the roads were mostly dry. We decided that Ronny and I would both follow in the team car. He would be on the radio, his usual role, and I gave him information to convey to the team. The course was slightly downhill and very fast, following wide, smooth roads along a valley in the shadow of snow-capped peaks. At 53 kilometres it was a relatively long team time trial and we knew we had to pace it carefully. Go out too hard and you risked losing riders prematurely.

The Wiggle High5 team did exactly that. They were fastest at the first intermediate checkpoint, at 22 kilometres. Meanwhile Canyon//SRAM Racing were doing me proud. I could see all that preparation and all those practice sessions paying off. Although the course was fairly long, it was also mainly downhill so the girls could bowl along at well over 50 kilometres per hour. Their discipline was great and their changes were as smooth as a well-drilled team-pursuit squad. Our strategy was to ride cautiously for the first 20 kilometres, then tighten the screw in the second section.

We were riding to our plan, but Wiggle High5 were going surprisingly quick. Here was a team of women motivated by the knowledge that their team was going to fold at the end of the season, and a strong ride at these World Championships might help to secure a contract for them for next year.

The first time check was at 22.8 kilometres. Wiggle High5 went through in 25:34, an average speed of 53 kilometres per hour. A few minutes later our team clocked 25:44, 10 seconds slower. Not disastrous, but not ideal either. And there were still three more teams to come through the time check, including the defending champions, the powerful German team Sunweb. In the car Ronny pulled a face, as if to say, that's okay, I can handle that. The mechanic, Jochen, (who was sitting in the back clutching a set of wheels) and I made vaguely positive noises. The tension in that car was thick. Rationally we all knew that closing a 10-second gap over 30 kilometres was very achievable – if nothing went wrong.

Then it all started to go wrong for Wiggle High5. First Katie Archibald, one of Great Britain's star track riders, dropped off the back. Then the Swede Emilia Fahlin dropped away. A team's finishing time was based on the fourth rider to cross the line, so the riders in the Wiggle squad knew they could not afford to drop anyone. One of the quartet, Annette Edmondson, was really struggling to hang on to the wheels, so the other three had to check their speed to protect her.

As the road curved past Alpine meadows, in the shadow of rocky cliffs and steep wooded slopes, the sun began to creep out from behind the clouds. We were still riding to plan and, encouragingly, there were no signs that any of our riders were tiring prematurely. In the team car, we listened to the race radio that gave occasional bursts of information amid a lot of unintelligible crackle. In front of us, the team's rear disc wheels made a rhythmic beating sound. On an open stretch of road beside a train track, the team that had started three minutes ahead of us came into sight. Having something to aim at always helps in time trials. It gives you that extra incentive to increase the speed, to make the catch. I could sense the team ratchet up the pace just a little. On a slightly downhill section the women moved across to the left and stormed past the other team, who looked disorganised and unhappy in comparison. Just as that happened a colourful local train zipped past all of us.

As Wiggle High5 came into the outskirts of Innsbruck, they began to adopt the Mehdi Method, with Annette Edmondson playing the role of Tipper – leaving a gap in front of her for the front rider to drop into. Doing this helped them to stay together to the finish in the centre of Innsbruck where they recorded 1:02.43, the fastest time at that point.

As we neared the finish it was obvious we would blast away the time set by Wiggle High5. With three kilometres remaining we were nearly a minute faster. Alongside the River Inn the road twisted down towards the finish. Still we had all six riders together. On a short rise, with two kilometres remaining, one rider, Alena Amialiusik, dropped behind. With five riders still in the line and only a short distance to the finish, she could have eased up and let the team ride away. But she dug deep into her reserves of energy to accelerate and within 500 metres she had made it back to the rear wheel of the rider in front. Such was the team spirit, Amialiusik fought to get back and cross the line with her team-mates.

All six Canyon//SRAM Racing riders finished together, hurtling across the finish line with a time of 1:01.47, an average speed of just under 53 kilometres per hour. As the girls sat slumped on the tarmac, trying to recover from their deep effort, Ronny and I nervously watched the three remaining teams from the team car (which is fitted with a small television screen). But those last three teams couldn't get near our time. When the final team's time ticked past our own time, and they still had 200 metres to race, Ronny and I jumped around in our seats like lunatics, punching the roof of the car and yelling a mix of German and English celebrations. I was elated. That moment was a release of pure pent-up energy. Only then did I realise how much the whole project had meant to me. For days the nerves had been building and now all that adrenaline came flooding out.

Backstage at the medal ceremony, as the team got ready to step out on to the stage, Ronny told me I had to go out with them and take the applause of the crowd. The team were allowed one representative to go on the podium, and Ronny wanted it to be me to thank me for the work I had done. The girls were chattering excitedly, still reliving moments in the race, and I just tagged along behind. The good people of Innsbruck, plus a good portion of the cycling press, must have been wondering who this tall grinning Englishman was, lurking behind the team as they received their gold medals. Winning that World Championship was every bit as rewarding as winning with Team KGF. It was one of the most rewarding and enjoyable experiences of my life. I can remember nearly every turn of that course, who was on the front and where, and the time checks along the way. It is etched in my memory. I went home from Innsbruck buzzing with ideas for the future.

Ronny Lauke had been paying attention to what Team KGF had achieved, was modest enough to admit when he needed help, and was prepared to pay for that help. He valued what I brought to his team, and his operation was small enough to be able to adapt. Women's road teams, while their budgets are bigger than Team KGF's budget, still operate on a very lean business model. There is no governance, no management hierarchy, no administration. Just a tight team who want to win and are flexible enough to do whatever that takes. Much like Team KGF, this group of women and their coaches could try new ideas, make decisions on the ground, and quickly create positive feedback loops to gauge the success of what they tried. Ronny had effectively done his reverse engineering homework. He knew what kind of performance it would take to win the World Championship and he knew that his riders were capable of it. He also knew that his missing link was specialist knowledge, and that is where I fitted in.

The reverse engineering approach can also work in scenarios where no benchmark of high performance has previously been set. In a new type of competition, all you need is to be able to estimate what level of performance will give the result you want.

In 2020, during the early days of the Covid-19 crisis, I worked again with Ronny and the Canyon//SRAM Racing women. This time the situation was very new to everyone. Cycle racing was prohibited during the lockdown. Very quickly, racing moved online. Virtual racing, mostly using the Zwift platform, had been around for several years but was used mainly as a training tool for 'real' racing. Very few took it too seriously, especially the professionals, who were generally quite scornful of it. Suddenly every racing cyclist who needed their fix of competition was checking the strength of their broadband connection.

The set-up was relatively simple: first lock a bike on to a stationary trainer. Referred to as turbo trainers, these machines have a solid metal frame to prevent unwanted movement. The bike's front wheel rests on the floor while the rear wheel sits on an electromagnetic flywheel, which offers resistance and enables the turbo trainer to measure the power a rider is putting out. Second, the rider connects the turbo trainer to the racing platform via Bluetooth and enters a specific event. Place a screen in front of the rider and he or she can see themselves competing on a virtual course (which is often a representation of a famous bike race) with competitors from all over the world.

Faced with being unable to run their events on the road, the more progressive race organisers took their races online, inviting the same professional riders. My role with Canyon//SRAM Racing was to help them prepare for these virtual races. Professional teams had never been involved in this world, so there was no established way of doing things. My approach was, of course, to reverse engineer the event. We knew roughly the kind of power output that would produce a race-winning ride, so we could work backwards from that measurable objective. And as we dismantled the event we could foresee the kind of challenges and opportunities that this new form of racing would entail.

It was important to remind the riders that this was different to racing on the road, and consequently had its own set of challenges and opportunities. For example, when riding stationary, there is no wind to cool you down. Even if you move the turbo trainer out into the garden, you're still not moving, so you're going to get very hot very quickly and lose a lot of fluid through sweating. This will result in sub-optimal performance and dehydration. So we adopted pre-cooling strategies such as slushy drinks, positioning multiple fans around the riders, pre-cooled drinks and menthol gels. I also worked with the team's nutritionist to calculate how much water the riders should be drinking during the race, and which electrolytic supplements to add to their bottles. We agreed that it was important to educate the riders on this subject, to empower them with the scientific reasons for what we were proposing.

Equipment choice became critical. Zwift designed their platform to replicate the physical and technical challenges of road cycling as closely as possible. We used direct drive turbo trainers, which operate with the rear wheel removed. As the rider pedals her power goes straight into the machine, and is recorded with a high degree of accuracy. The system is calibrated to use a virtual weight, aerodynamics and rolling resistance for each rider and we developed a system to test all our virtual equipment options before the racing. Because no one had used Zwift to this level of preparation before, there were a lot of unknowns. We just kept prodding it to see what happened.

Then there are the tactics. While the platform aims to replicate the tactical dynamics of road racing, inevitably it has its own quirks. The riders needed to understand these before they got into a race situation; if they were learning during the race itself they'd be putting themselves under unnecessary mental stress. We also had a specific staff member watching the Zoom live-stream cameras to keep track of rider fatigue, in both our own riders and others, so that I could direct our race strategy accordingly. Using Zwift and Zoom gives a team manager so much more information to act upon.

There will always be some things out of our control. During the 2020 Zwift racing season, one of our riders was in with a shout of winning a major race with 10 kilometres to go when her broadband connection dropped out, freezing her screen. When she was finally able to get reconnected this 'mechanical' meant she had dropped far behind the other riders. Cue a lot of angry emojis on the team's WhatsApp chat.

* * *

The transition from athlete to coach is not often easy. Success as an athlete does not translate into guaranteed success as a coach. Former England rugby player Jonny Wilkinson has spoken at length about his own journey from star player to apprentice coach. Wilkinson recognised that his track record as a player, and his celebrity profile, did not give him the right to tell other players how to train and compete. Instead he approached coaching with humility and intelligence, taking time to listen and to educate himself. With the growing importance of science in sport, coaching has changed significantly in recent years. Whereas previously the coach would be the fount of all (often imperfect) knowledge, working alone with the athlete or team, now the coach plays a more generalist role. Elite athletes now benefit from the specialist knowledge of physiologists, psychologists, nutritionists, data analysts and other experts. The coach coordinates all these inputs and helps the athlete make sense of them.

Above all, a coach has to be a good communicator. Wilkinson developed this part of his skill set by spending time observing how England coaches worked in the run-up to international matches and by mentoring young players at his former club, Toulon. He recognised that understanding the mental and emotional aspects of your athletes is the foundation to unlocking their best performances. The pressure, for a coach, is different to that of an athlete. The athlete has the stress of performing. The coach has the stress of having to watch their athlete perform, unable to influence the result once the competition starts.

When I worked with Canyon//SRAM Racing, I was not a coach but one of the specialists brought in to focus on a specific aspect of performance. Nevertheless, working with Ronny and his team at those World Championships, and later on the Zwift project, gave me some insight into the world of being a coach. It showed me just how much I have yet to learn about leading a team. Science, engineering and following a process are all solid building blocks as we strive for success, but they mean nothing if the human element is omitted. Successful teams talk and listen to one another; they understand and support one another. That requires maturity, empathy, honesty and commitment from everyone. The end result may be a gold medal but there is a deeper satisfaction to be gained – that of working together.

24

Sport and innovation

Cycling is a very traditional sport, and there is much to appreciate in that. There is that strong sense of history, underpinned by the idea (which is really a delusion) that the sport is not really so different to the sport of 50 or even 100 years ago.

And cycling as a sport is complemented by cycling as a leisure activity. Everyone who races bikes also enjoys simply riding their bike – the freedom of escaping into the countryside with friends, or alone with one's thoughts. Professional riders, with all the stress and pressure of their job, sometimes lose sight of what they first loved about the sport. They get stale. Training becomes a chore. Just the sight of their bike makes them feel tired. When this happens, performance invariably dips. The answer to this problem is to find a way to rediscover the love for the bike. Give them some time to have fun and before you know it their Instagram posts will be genuinely joyful rather than just put together to please sponsors.

But the innocent pleasure of riding a bike is not mutually exclusive with technological developments. It is not an either/or situation. Indeed, cycling has always been pushed forward by technology and innovation. For much of the twentieth century this manifested itself as an obsession with lighter bikes. Over recent decades the focus has expanded to designing more aerodynamic bikes, gaining a better understanding of physiology through technology, training and nutrition. The Hour Record is a case in point. Throughout its history the distance cycled in one hour by the successful athletes has increased. In the last 50 years the record has seen technological innovation from Francesco Moser, Graeme Obree and Chris Boardman, until Boardman's 1996 distance prompted the reactionary cycling authorities to change the rules.

Technology can also explain much of the progress made in other sports. In athletics, when Roger Bannister broke the four-minute mile, he was running on cinders. Biomechanical studies have shown that this would have absorbed much more of his energy than the artificial surfaces laid down on running tracks today. In other words, he and many of his peers would have broken the four-minute mile much sooner had someone designed a better running track. Even in swimming, which seems to involve minimal technology, innovation has played a part. A swimming pool gutter does not sound like the most exciting piece of modern technology, but they reduce turbulence in the water and when they were first introduced, world records tumbled.

Technological innovation is an inherent part of sport, yet it is rarely celebrated. When a team or individual achieves something amazing in sport, it is the physical human endeavour that is lauded. Technology is recognised only as an afterthought, if at all. Partly this is because new technology is often hidden, either because teams want to maintain their competitive advantage, or simply because the media don't understand the detail (if some coaches are stuck in outdated ways of thinking, so too are many television commentators). But this late recognition is also because sport still has a rather queasy attitude to technology.

Those who are most embracing of technology are the athletes who stand to make a performance gain, and the brands who supply them with equipment. Forward-looking athletes want to work with forward-looking brands, those that want to keep pushing the boundaries of what their products can give to athletes. Of course, the brands are not doing this out of purely altruistic motives. They are motivated by increasing revenue through bringing new products to market. Elite athletes are the perfect guinea pigs for products in development, and (going one better than the proverbial guinea pig) responsive athletes can create positive feedback loops with those brands.

Beyond this pairing of brand and athlete, the response to innovation is more ambiguous. The media who cover sport want stories, and in stories we all respond to the human element. Narratives about physical achievements are simpler and, on the surface at least, more human, than narratives about complicated intellectual efforts behind the scenes. Our perception of sporting stories has been shaped by movies such as *Rocky*, in which an underdog prevails against a cold, cynical opponent through sheer tenacity and spirit. Or by *Cool Runnings*, in which a plucky bunch of Jamaican runners are transformed into a bobsleigh team for the Winter Olympics. We all love an underdog story but in the search for a dramatic story, innovation can get lost along the way. Let's face it, *Rocky* would not be as good as it is if the training sequences showed long hours sitting in front of a laptop analysing his footwork, instead of lifting logs above his head in a forest.

Our attitude to sport is still heavily influenced by the Olympic motto of *Citius, Altius, Fortius* – Faster, Higher, Stronger. There is no place for 'cleverer'. When Dick Fosbury brought his new high-jump technique to the 1968 Mexico Olympics, the world was captivated. Fosbury, from Oregon in the United States, invented the new technique because he was too tall to effectively use the other methods commonly practised at the time. The 'Fosbury Flop' maximised the impact of the primary resource he had – height. The advent of Fosbury's new technique was truly a landmark moment in athletics. Fosbury spent five years, starting at the age of 16, developing his new technique. An outstanding student of maths and physics, as well as an outstanding athlete, he understood the laws of physics that governed his event, principally gravity. By methodically testing different ideas, Fosbury's technique evolved, progressively gaining height. And technology played a role too. Before Fosbury began taking the high jump seriously, high-jump competitions had a landing pit constructed of sand or wood-chips. To land on your back on such a surface would likely have resulted in serious injury, so athletes used techniques that allowed them to land on their feet. This was a significant constraint on innovation. In the early 1960s, however, colleges around the United

States were installing deep foam landing pads. This simple piece of technology not only meant that Fosbury could use a technique that involved landing on his back, but also that he could practise and refine it over and over again, every day, without fear of injury.

In the twenty-first century, technology in sport is a lot more complicated than a foam landing pad. Governing bodies are often unsure of where to draw an ethical line between what constitutes technical development in their sport, and what constitutes cheating. They are also slow to react. This is something we have seen many times in cycling. If a company developed a new piece of kit, or a rider came up with a new position, it always seemed to blindside the UCI. They discussed it internally and, after a period of time, pronounced a judgement on whether that new piece of kit was allowed. There was no transparent process for making this judgement, nor was there any consultation.

In swimming, the line between technology and cheating became confused in the aftermath of the 2008 Beijing Olympics. For the Games, Speedo created the LZR Racer swimsuit. This all-in-one swimsuit was so advanced that Speedo had worked on it with NASA. It had three significant benefits for the swimmer: better flow of blood to the muscles, better hydrodynamics (the equivalent of aerodynamics in water) and increased buoyancy through trapping air. At Beijing and in subsequent competitions, swimmers wearing the LZR Racer broke many world records. Eventually the sport's governing body banned it.

When the Royal Netherlands Football Association (KNVB) first developed the Video Assistant Referee (VAR) in 2012, FIFA were very reluctant to incorporate it into international football, particularly their flagship event, the World Cup. The system aims to reduce human error among referees by providing video evidence and two-way communication between the referee and a team of experts reviewing the video footage. Similar systems had been used in rugby for many years previously, yet the idea was considered controversial in football, with traditionalists claiming it would destroy the spirit of the game. The KNVB trialled the system in friendly matches in the Netherlands, then petitioned the sport's global governing bodies to amend their rules to allow other countries to stage trials. Over the next four years the top-flight club leagues in the United States, Spain, Germany and Italy began to introduce VAR. Glitches were resolved, the methodology was refined, and when VAR was finally introduced to the World Cup, in 2018, it was a success.

Here is an example of technological innovation being integrated into a sport by a governing body in a considered, planned way with lots of testing and consensus-building. It was also successful because it did not especially benefit any one team. Yet even this entirely sensible idea was subject to the emotional response of the person in charge of FIFA. Sepp Blatter, the president of FIFA between 1998 and 2015, was firmly against the introduction of the technology, despite a growing tide of opinion in the football world that it made sense to use technology to avoid mistaken decisions. Blatter claimed that football needed to retain a human face, and even that debate over contentious refereeing decisions was a feature of the game to be upheld. The matter was solved when Blatter was suspended from FIFA in 2015 under a cloud of corruption allegations. His successor was more progressive in his thinking and VAR was introduced to the World Cup.

With the advent of big tech companies such as Amazon and Google, innovation has become something of a buzzword. But innovation means different things to different companies. And not every company *needs* to innovate in the same way. It depends on the market you are in. Innovation for a chain of bookshops is going to look very different to innovation for a mobile phone manufacturer. Ultimately it always come back to meeting consumer needs.

Failure to get behind innovation can lead to a company's demise. In the early nineties Borders was a giant of book retailing in the United States. It had over 500 huge stores and 19,500 employees. When Amazon came along in the late nineties, Borders took no action. When Amazon became a serious player in the market, Borders decided to outsource its online operation to Amazon. This may have seemed like a clever decision – using Amazon's operation to deliver easy sales – but in the long run Borders damaged their brand and lost customers to a key competitor. While Amazon continued to grow, and other competitors such as Barnes & Noble invested in online platforms, Borders stuck their head in the sand. All their investment was focused on their big, and increasingly unprofitable, physical stores. They continued to stock CDs and DVDs long after their competitors had switched focus to digital products. In 2011 they went into liquidation. Former CEO Mike Edwards later said, "I think you have to face the digital impact head-on and not go through denial. You can't rely on past tactics to change the trajectory of the company, because it doesn't work any more."

The leadership of Borders lacked the courage to embrace innovations that were making long-term structural shifts in their industry, and the company eventually paid the price. Mobile phone giant Nokia also failed to recognise innovations that were becoming increasingly important to its industry, but for different cultural reasons to Borders. One of the first generation of mobile phone manufacturers, in 2007 Nokia was earning over 50 per cent of all profits from mobile phone sales. The Finnish company started out in 1865 as a pulp mill, then diversified into rubber and cabling, before moving into electronics and telecommunications in the 1970s. Nokia's first mobile phone prototypes were produced in the early 1980s and the company invested heavily in research and development.

Their problems began when Apple and Samsung began producing smartphones. Nokia's corporate culture was dominated by hardware engineers. They understood how to make a great device, but the software to run on that device was not a focus. Apple and Samsung placed equal importance on software and hardware. Apple, in particular, developed a culture of total integration between software and hardware. Products were designed in multi-disciplinary teams. Nokia mistakenly thought that smartphones were not worth investing in, because they would only appeal to a relatively small market. They also thought that their brand was so strong, and the physical build of their devices so robust, that consumers would remain loyal. Another big mistake; modern consumers are promiscuous. By 2010 Nokia had fallen behind Apple and Samsung and when it tried to develop its smartphone products, the innovation came too late. In 2013, when Nokia sold its handset business to

Microsoft, it had just 3 per cent of the global mobile phone market. An ironic footnote to the Nokia story is that in 2017 the company updated and reissued their classic 3310 handset. Among the slew of expensive and complicated smartphones on the market, the 3310 stood out as a much simpler option for people who only wanted to use their phone for calling and texting. Its primary selling features were how long the battery lasted, and the nice feel of its chunky buttons. The new 3310 proved popular among older people who didn't want, or couldn't understand, a smartphone. Which goes to prove that innovation can look backwards as well as ahead.

Coming back to reverse engineering, Nokia demonstrated what happens when you do not set ambitious goals. They failed to understand the future of their industry and so their development was limited to improving their existing proposition. Consequently they did not seek to understand their competition, instead basing their assumptions only on their own past performance.

In the business world, then, a failure to get behind innovation can have various root causes. Usually those causes have less to do with ethical lines being crossed – the concern for sport's governing bodies – and more to do with corporate cultures that fear or withstand change.

Technological development is unstoppable. Innovation in sport should not be held back because innovation is intrinsically part of sport, indeed intrinsically a part of human life. If a team pursuit team win a world title because their engineers have decreased their drag, that should be applauded. The direction of interactive technology, such as augmented reality, means that fans will soon be able to see and understand a lot more about the science involved in athletic performance. Much of the innovation in sports in recent years has been in systems that are invisible to fans: electronic chips in football boots that allow analysts to track players around a pitch, virtual reality training simulations that give a football team the opportunity to train against their rivals, genetic testing to ascertain which event a young athlete is suited to, and wearable tech that is tailored to the demands of specific events. These innovations are not only helping athletes perform better, they are helping us better understand physiology and biomechanics.

As a sport, Formula One understands that its USP is its marriage of human endeavour (driver) and engineering (car). We could also characterise this as the marriage of physical and intellectual. I would like to see cycling and other sports adopt an approach like that, rather than trying to hide behind tradition and the myth of superhuman sportsmen.

One benefit of a more open attitude to innovation is the trickle-down of new ideas to aspiring athletes. In cycling, take any young racer and he or she will have a far more sophisticated grasp of aerodynamics (and all the other variables of performance) than a Tour de France winner 30 years ago would have done. Unlike Formula One, innovative cycling kit is available to anyone to purchase at a relatively affordable level.

Even club cyclists, who might never pin a number on to their backs, can benefit from some aerodynamic improvements. At only 15 miles per hour, more energy is used breaking through the air than on the rolling resistance of tyres on tarmac. That is why bike manufacturers are marketing their road bikes as 'aero'. They know that club cyclists love to imitate the professionals, but there are also genuine benefits for them too. The next step will be for mainstream bike computer companies like Garmin to start building aerodynamic metrics like CdA into their data collection. It may seem unnecessary for your average leisure cyclist to be keeping an eye on his CdA during a Sunday morning ride, but when he gets to that final hill and has more energy left than his mates, it will suddenly seem very important.

Innovation is at the heart of reverse engineering. As we dismantle something, innovation can help us to understand. And as we build our own plans towards success, innovation gives us more options to get there. Nurture the attitude of the innovator in yourself. Whatever your goal, there are always new roads to pedal along to get there.

Acknowledgements

It turns out that writing a book is a team effort as much as riding a bike race. I would like to thank my editor Oli Holden-Rea, my agent James Spackman, and Paul Maunder for steering me away from filling the book with spreadsheets. He wasn't convinced by "every spreadsheet tells a story". My career so far would have been impossible without the friendship, insight and support of the many talented people I have worked with over the years. Firstly my team-mates: Jacob Tipper, Jonny Wale, Charlie Tanfield, Harry Tanfield, John Archibald, Ashton Lambie, Will Perrett, Kyle Gordon, Ethan Vernon, Si Wilson & George Peasgood. My road team managers for being so supportive of my wild ideas and requests, Jack Rees and Tom Timothy.

The partners who have supported us, who are absolutely vast in their numbers, but specifically Dean Jackson for his ambition and drive to help, Mehdi Kordi, Steve Faulkner, Lewis Gough and Kurt Bergin-Taylor for their blind faith and support in us chasing our lofty sporting ambitions, Mark Akers and Rich Steels for keeping our bikes just about legal, Becky Davies for supporting at every race practically possible all around the world, Adam Wade and Rich Needham for their commitment to doing every task asked of them, and Ellie Green for being eternally helpful and positive, no matter the issue or challenge.

262 | Start at the End

The teams I have worked with: Canyon//SRAM Racing, Jumbo Visma and the Danish Cycle Union. The Union Cycliste Internationale, for giving us the opportunity to innovate through your endless regulation changes.

There are many dedicated writers, photographers and videographers who have helped to tell our story: the eternally present Larry Hickmott, James Poole, Oli Hutton, James Huntly, Kenza Barton-Schlee, Gary Main, Vern Pitt, William Fotheringham, Oliver Bridgewood, and many more. Thank you for letting me speak at length and say all sorts of things I probably shouldn't.

Finally I'd like to thank my mother, father and brothers for their unstinting support for my crazy schemes. And to my better half, Joss. For feeding me, watering me and taking me for walks. You're really something special, I would recommend anyone writing a book to have a Joss Lowden on tap.